Nov. 1, 1993

Aloha,

Les Keiter

FIFTY YEARS BEHIND THE MICROPHONE

The Les Keiter Story

FIFTY YEARS BEHIND THE MICROPHONE

The Les Keiter Story

Les Keiter

With Dennis Christianson

A Kolowalu Book

UNIVERSITY OF HAWAII PRESS
Honolulu

To Lila

©1991 University of Hawaii Press
All rights reserved.
Printed in the United States of America
91   92   93   94   95   96   5   4   3   2   1

Library of Congress Cataloging-In-Publication Data
Keiter, Les, 1919-
    Fifty years behind the microphone: the Les Keiter story / by Les
Keiter; with Dennis Christianson
        p. cm. —(A Kolowalu book)
    Includes index.
    ISBN 0-8248-1388-X
    1. Keiter, Les, 1919– . 2. Sportscasters—United States—
Biography. I. Christianson, Dennis. II. Title. III. 50 years behind the
microphone.
    GV742.42.K45A3 1991
    070.4´49796´092—dc 20
    [B]   91-8217
                                        CIP

Photographs and illustrations are from the collection of Les Keiter and are
used with his permission.

Design, production and publishing services provided by Laing
Communications Inc., Redmond, Washington.

University of Hawaii Press books are printed on acid-free paper and meet
the guidelines for permanence and durablility of the Council on Library
Resources.

Contents

Prologue—The Summer of '28

IT IS A SCENE that has no doubt been played by countless youngsters around countless campfires many times over the last seven or more decades:

A group of young boys, a dozen or so, attending a summer camp, sharing their dreams and plans for life as a grownup, prodded along by a much-admired camp counselor. This camp happened to be in western Washington State, a place called Orkila (the camp name was spelled Orcila until 1939).

One child wants to be a fireman. Another a policeman. One wants to be a carpenter so he can build things for people. A different boy plans to work at a newspaper, just like his father. Finally, the counselor asks young Lester what he wants to do when he grows up.

The boy doesn't hesitate for a moment.

"When I grow up," he tells them, "I'm going to be a sports broadcaster in Yankee Stadium, in New York!"

Not I *want* to. Not I *plan* to. I'm *going* to. There isn't the least bit of doubt in his voice. He has a dream, and he intends to see it come true.

Some thirty years later, a vastly different scene:

A much larger group, tens of thousands of somewhat older boys—adults, in as much as any sports fan is an adult—gathered around not a campfire but a boxing ring, awaiting the arrival of the contender and champion for a world heavyweight title bout.

The place is Yankee Stadium in the Bronx, New York City.

An announcer sits at ringside, preparing for the fight. But just before the opening bell, he is handed a telegram. It is from one Charlie Norman of Seattle, Washington, the superintendent of the YMCA in that city. The telegram reads:

DEAR LES KEITER.

WE REMEMBER A NINE-YEAR-OLD BOY SAYING AT CAMPFIRE, "SOMEDAY, I'M GOING TO BROADCAST FROM YANKEE STADIUM."

TONIGHT, WE ARE ALL LISTENING TO YOU DO IT. CONGRATULATIONS.

That's the closest thing to clairvoyance I've ever managed. And even then I messed it up—I had expected to be doing a baseball game, not a heavyweight fight. In fact, I never would get the chance to do play-by-play for the Yankees.

But I did just about everything else.

And I had a great time doing it.

The Early Years

*The kid who was born to be
a sports broadcaster*

IT REALLY BEGAN far from arenas or ballparks, television or
radio studios.

The Les Keiter story was formulated in the incomparable
islands of the San Juan Archipelago. I came into this world the
son of proud parents Jake and Ruth Keiter, April 27, 1919. They
were wonderful people and wonderful parents. My parents moved
to Seattle, Washington, from Chicago in 1916 along with the
Birnbaums—my Uncle Joe and Aunt Effie—to found the first
Keiter and Birnbaum Cigar Store in the old Savoy Hotel on
Second Avenue. Keiter and Birnbaum became a minor downtown landmark in Seattle. It was the kind of establishment you
don't find much of anymore, the kind with the tobacco and candy
counter up front, the long restaurant bar (with a well-known
Japanese cook, known only as "Joe"), a row of high-backed
booths that made it a popular place for business lunches, and a
card room in the back where some of Seattle's prominent citi-

zens would drop in, ostensibly for lunch, and then mosey into the card room to play for an hour or two. Maybe pinochle, maybe rummy. I never knew.

Mother was born Ruth Silverman, but before she was even a teenager she had picked up the nickname "Dolly," which would stay with her all her life.

I'm sure I was a delightful baby, though the record book on my early seasons is sketchy. No one knew then that I would talk my way into the major arenas and ballparks of the country, and indeed, by the time I was four, I was well on the way to talking myself into another kind of institution altogether. It is my shame to admit that before even beginning kindergarten, I was almost incorrigible.

The Keiter family resided in Seattle's Montlake District. Our house happened to be on a streetcar line—a delight for a precocious youngster. One of my favorite activities was to hide behind a big bush just off the sidewalk in front of our house and then dash out to pile my toys right in the middle of the streetcar tracks. Then, back in hiding, I happily watched the city transit system come to a grinding halt as the conductor was forced to stop the trolley, get out of the car, and move my toys to the sidewalk before resuming his journey. It was great sport until the day my chagrined parents were visited by company officials and told that if future transgressions occurred, the family would be forced to move.

I was confined to the yard.

Not that a mere incident with the City of Seattle would keep me down. There were other frontiers to conquer. Dad put in (at considerable cost) an expensive six-foot-high fence to keep me from wandering off. I loved to leave the yard unescorted as I looked for adventures on my way to my aunt and uncle's home several blocks away. Unfortunately, Dad and Mom simply did not take into account the ingenuity and innovative powers of their little guy. I quickly found a new use for the roadblocking toys. Not twenty-four hours after the fence's completion, I had stacked the toys into a completely serviceable escape ladder over the new backyard fence and bye-bye baby! I was off into the neighborhood again to visit my cousins.

How proud my parents must have been!

We moved to a new home in the Capitol Hill District just in time for the arrival of my little brother, George Edward, born December 17, 1923. When told I now had a little brother, my

Even at age three I exhibited signs of a radio broadcaster—an open mouth.

pronunciation of brother became buddy—he was my buddy. That is still what I call him today. One day, ever anxious to please, I decided to surprise my mother, who was busy doing the family wash, by bringing brother Buddy down to visit her in the basement. Carefully, I removed him from his crib and carried him down two flights of stairs to the living room and then to the laundry room—holding baby the entire journey securely by the head. Mother took it quite calmly, considering her doubtless inner panic when she saw us strolling down the stairs. I have kidded my brother ever since about the brain damage I must have caused.

And there was more.

I threw the family cat in the fireplace; Dad rescued it. Later, the same poor feline was tossed into the toilet (and thankfully survived a flushing). At age six, I liberated several prized bottles of genuine Scotch whiskey (this was during Prohibition), and poor Father arrived in the bathroom just in time to see the last drops being poured into the commode. When he gasped, I turned and uttered the immortal words "Foo-foo water, Daddy!" as the last two glurgs left the bottle. An amazing child!

Mother was understandably concerned at letting me loose among other children at elementary school, but to everyone's surprise (though frankly, I don't recall my feelings at the time) I did just fine, and with the exception of a typical childish zeal for pranks (doesn't everyone lock themselves in the bathroom with a two-year-old brother and a screaming babysitter after calling in a false fire alarm at the house?), I became a model student. My parents' relief is unrecorded, but assumed.

My grades were more than adequate, but like most young-sters, my passions were found mostly outside the classroom—baseball, football, and other kid games including, of all things, something called "roller-hockey." We had a regular roller-hockey league that played on a street three blocks from my house. (Not too many years ago, Roger Melrose, the headmaster of Seabury Hall, a private school on Maui, wrote me to ask if I remembered the roller-hockey games in Seattle; he and his brother played against me and my brother!) And starting at about age nine, a portion of every summer was spent at a place that to this day is still close to my heart—Camp Orkila, on Orcas Island.

Camp Orkila was (and still is) operated by the Seattle-area YMCA. They also had what was called "Friendly Indian Camp" for younger kids, six to eight years old, on Seattle's beautiful Lake Washington. Attendance at Camp Orkila proper began at age nine. The summer was divided into five two-week sessions for kids from the different areas of the city—University District, Queen Anne District, the Central District, and so on. After my first year, my parents signed me up for several sessions, so I would spend the better part of my summer break there. I'm sure it was like most other YMCA or Boy Scout camps, with nature studies, leathercraft, swimming, canoeing, and countless other sports activities. There were overnight hikes. There was a roughed-in amphitheater called Chapel Rock, where we had Sunday services in which this nice Jewish boy participated en-thusiastically. Though I remember them now as mature, older role models, most of the counselors were in fact quite young, and I still recall most of them by name. Some of my dearest, lifelong friends were kids I met at Orkila—Pearce Smith, Bill Code, Doug Paul, Bill Slater, Bud Collins, Knute Qvale, Bob Schaeffer, and many more. We were also involved in wintertime camp reunions. In short, Orkila was a simply wonderful place. It was run by a man named Charles G. Norman. It was he who sent the telegram to me three decades later, at my Yankee Stadium debut.

My prime interest in those years was softball. I played the game until I developed blisters, and then I played some more. I actually had to go home one summer because a blister broke open, and I developed blood poisoning. I couldn't get enough of the sport and darned near lived at the camp ballpark. Everyone there knew it. I helped build a new backstop. We planted grass. One summer we even erected a left-field fence, which saved us the chore of chasing the ball into the woods. When we couldn't get enough guys together for a proper game, we played a "home run" version with three kids on a team. God, I just loved it!

Every Sunday our parents came to visit. The ballpark served as a parking lot for the camp visitors. The Keiters were famous for bringing huge bags of fresh corn on the cob for the whole camp to enjoy at the Sunday picnic dinners. And each session of the summer there were the famous "All-Stars vs. Leaders" softball games that would pit the camper all-stars against the camp counselors, with fifty-year-old Charlie Norman as pitcher. It was heaven for me, and years later, during my stint in the

We erect the new baseball backstop at Camp Orkila. Camp Director Charlie Norman is on the ladder. The field is now called Keiter Park.

Navy, I learned that the Orkila ballfield was renamed Keiter Park, complete with an engraved plaque. A rare honor.

It was my first year at Orkila when Charlie Norman launched the tradition of each camper standing by the final night's fire to describe his goals and plans for the future. I don't know if they still do that up there, but it would be nice to think that they do.

So I was about that same age—eight or nine—when I developed my second interest in sports, namely, broadcasting.

I loved listening to Leo Lassen, the dean of Seattle sportscasters, and his coverage of the Seattle Indians (later the Rainiers) of the Pacific Coast League. There were no major league teams on the West Coast then; this was decades before the Dodgers and Giants left New York for California. Leo Lassen was as much a childhood hero for me as any ballplayer, and eventually I earned a reputation doing imitations of him. My parents gave me a baseball board game that used three dice to determine hits, strikeouts, and so on; as I recall, three fours were a double, three fives were a triple, and three sixes a homer. As I played the game, I would describe the action in my best Lassen soundalike voice. I began to make up ball games, announcing them from my own imagination, and even kept scorebooks of the imaginary competitions. Those scorebooks were around for years; eventually my mother must have thrown them out. But the damage was already done. By age nine, I knew I wanted to be a sports broadcaster.

After Seward Elementary School I moved on to Broadway High, where I was once again a good enough student but an even more enthusiastic ballplayer. Unfortunately, enthusiasm wasn't enough for the varsity baseball coach, A. J. Johnson. I was lost in anonymity on the team. I'd sit on the bench, not playing in the games and considering quitting because I wasn't getting any playing time. I began to think that the coach had forgotten all about me until one day a foul ball was knocked over a fence onto the busy Broadway street, and he turned and yelled, "Keiter, go get that ball!" I suppose I should have been humiliated, but after all those weeks of being ignored, I was appreciative of the recognition. My perseverance finally paid off. Shortly thereafter I made the starting team.

I made a lot of lifelong friends playing ball while I was growing up: Eddie Guthman, later a Pulitzer Prize–winning author and international editor for the *Los Angeles Times*, editor of

The Philadelphia Inquirer, and press secretary to Bobby Kennedy; Dewey Soriano, who became president of the Seattle Pilots, Seattle's first expansion entry in the American League; the late Freddie Hutchinson, who became a Cincinnati Reds manager; Phil Evans, Jim Hjelm, Herm Blumenthal, Marion Kindred, and the list goes on and on.

Football was also a favorite, though my parents didn't like the violent aspects of the game. I was persuaded not to go out for Broadway High's varsity team, but this promise was neatly circumvented by my participation in a neighborhood football league, a league I in part helped organize. Our team was the Roanoke Park Rats, named after a lovely neighborhood park, and we played other neighborhood sandlot teams—Gene Cotton's Greeks, cross-town rivals Scott's Garfield Stars, and several others. We were a hard-nosed bunch and managed to win most of our games. The competition was intense enough to earn a few newspaper write-ups.

We didn't have the proper equipment or coaching as we might have had in an organized league, but it was football, and a way for me to get around my parents. I played into my fresh-

Rats Run Amok!

Featuring a hard charging line and a tricky offense, the Roanoke Rats trounced Fred Roger's Capitol Hill Eleven, 24–0, at Montlake Field. The Rats scored early when captain Les Keiter went seventeen yards around end to pay dirt. A few plays later Roanoke scored again on a pass from Bill Vogue to left end Ed Guthman. Recovering Keiter's fumble of the second-half kickoff, Guthman ran sixty-five yards behind perfect blocking to score. Vogue completed the scoring by going over from the two-yard line after the Rats had made a sustained drive of forty yards. Keiter was the outstanding man on the field both on offense and defense, while Marion Kindred, Phil Evans, and Kenny Heiman contributed to the win.

The Broadway High Whims, October 1937

man year at the University of Washington, and—parents or no—
I was determined to go out for the varsity team the next season. Then an ironic situation developed: I broke my shoulder
playing for the Rats, due in part to the lack of proper equipment.
My buddy, Eddie Guthman, drove me home from the game. I
was so doubled up with pain I couldn't fit into the car and had
to ride on the running board, holding on with my good right
arm. My dear dad was watering the lawn when we pulled up,
and with a single look at me—I had hoped for at least a sympathetic greeting—Dad turned and walked away down the sidewalk, swearing. Mother was nearly hysterical; her worst fear of
football was realized. Dad eventually came back, still swearing
to himself, and had me call "Click" Clark, the football trainer
at the University. Clark told my father to bring me down for
some x-rays. Alternately lecturing me ("I told you this would
happen; you know you were supposed to stay away from sandlot
football!" etc.) and muttering under his breath (worth quoting,
but unprintable), we drove to the University infirmary. I was
patched up as well as possible, but it was months before I had
full use of my arm again. I would never play football again,
though I had shown some promise as a running back. My father
was right. It was a stupid thing to do.

I was able to play baseball, though it was darn near a non-
spectator sport at the University of Washington. No one, but no
one, bothered to waste a good Washington spring day by coming out to watch college baseball. But I had a great time—baseball would always be my favorite game—and my Zeta Beta Tau
fraternity brothers came out to support our team and invited more
and more friends to join them.

Their interest wasn't entirely sports-motivated, however.
They came for an additional attraction. The team's left-fielder
did a play-by-play description of the very game in which he
was playing! The pitches, the strikes, the hits, everything except
his own at-bats! Guess who? It was the same kid who played
with dice and made up his own games, doing the same Leo
Lassen imitation, but with a hint of his own style creeping in.

My interest in sports and broadcasting kept growing all
through college, which did not really please my parents. They
wanted to see me in business or law. They already knew how
much I could talk; why waste it on the radio when I could do
it for a jury and make a decent living? They just couldn't see
me, or anyone for that matter, making a career out of something

like sportscasting. Of course, they only wanted the best for me.

During my sophomore year at the University, Dad and a longtime family friend, Al Barker, arranged a weekend job for me helping out in the men's suit department at Rhodes Department Store, across the street from Jake's Cigar Store. Dad saw it as a kind of vocational experiment, I suppose. As for me, I took the job for the pocket money. Friday nights I was just fine, a model employee. Unfortunately, on Saturdays all the big college football games were on the radio, and it was nearly impossible for me to concentrate on my work. I would find any excuse to visit the tailor's room in the back, the location of the only radio on the premises, and my visits there tended to be longer rather than shorter. Mr. Barker caught me more times than not, and bless him, he did his level best to make me a salesman. It just wasn't meant to be. Finally, he went to my dad and said, "Jake, we are kidding ourselves, both of us. Lester is not going to become a salesmen of suits or anything else. His future is in sports and working on the radio. That's where his heart is. I'm sure I'm not telling you something you and Dolly don't already know." And so my business career came to an end.

My parents, in their hearts, must have known all along from the softball games at Camp Orkila and the dice games in my bedroom, from the dislocated joints and self-narrated games, and from the way my ears were always cocked to a tuned-in radio and the voices of Leo Lassen, Bill Stern, Ted Husing, and Harry Wismer. It was in my blood (Dad had been a hell of an athlete in his youth and was even asked to try out for the Chicago White Sox). Slowly, begrudgingly, my parents began to acknowledge the inevitable: their Lester was going to be a sports broadcaster.

And I intended to be a darn good one.

Big Guy Meets Little Guy

War, my brother, and an interview
with Gene Tunney

I GRADUATED FROM THE University of Washington in June 1941, and I was already a veteran radio announcer. Well, maybe that's overstating it a bit. I had managed to follow up my retail sales career fiasco with something closer to my heart: working part-time during my senior year at a local radio station, assisting the people who *really* worked there. It was a beginning. But now, with a brand-new sheepskin soon to be under my arm, I was ready for my career to begin in earnest.

But how? Jake and Dolly were dubious.

The spring before graduation our family went vacationing in a god-awful place in eastern Washington called Soap Lake. It's a resort, but it's in the gloomiest surroundings imaginable. I don't know why in the world we went there. I guess the folks liked it for some mineral baths or something, but believe me, there was nothing there. My brother and I—young specimens of budding manhood that we were—were bored to tears. Most of our time was spent sitting around the resort's swimming pool, which is precisely where my professional career commenced.

There was another family there from Spokane, and the father turned out to be one of the leading citizens of that city, Mr. Oscar Levitch. Our two families were chatting one afternoon at poolside, and I mentioned that I was about to graduate from the University of Washington, and I was interested in sports and radio. Mr. Levitch then proceeded to tell my father and mother and me that he knew all the radio people in Spokane, in particular Lou Wasmer, who owned KHQ/KGA Radio, the Red and Blue ABC Network affiliates there. "If Lester would come stay with us for the weekend, I'll introduce him to Lou Wasmer." My parents thought it was wonderful that this nice man was going to help launch their son's career. As for me, ungrateful hotshot that I was, I thought it was all a bunch of hot air. We left them with a "we'll be in touch," and I never expected to hear from him again.

Well, shame on me. Oscar Levitch was as good as his word. Just two weeks later I got a long-distance phone call from him. "Are you ready to come and spend the weekend with us?" I was and I went. Mr. Levitch was a *very* big man in Spokane. He owned a jewelry store the size of a small stadium. He *did* know all the sports and radio people. He *had* set up a meeting with Lou Wasmer's staff. Two days later, I had a job as a summer relief announcer on KGA Radio in Spokane, starting after my graduation the next month.

I was launched. On July 1, 1941, I was officially on-the-air. Thank you, Oscar. I never should have doubted you!

My job duties were modest enough. I read the program notes between shows, did the news breaks, station identifications, and so on. The money was just as modest, but I had no rent to pay, nor did I need money for meals: the Levitches insisted I stay with them. It was all a wonderful break for a kid just out of college. But all was not rosy. I had been on the job for only three or four days when the program director called me into his office. "You'll never make it in this business," he told me. "If I were you, I'd learn to drive a truck or something." But I knew I had an iron-clad, two-month contract for July and August. I was safe for seven more weeks, and I intended to make the most of them.

Fortunately, there was at least one person who didn't share the program director's views of my burgeoning skills. That person would prove to be more important to my career than any other man I've ever known.

I had been on the KGA airwaves for a few weeks when I got a phone call from Centralia, Washington. I didn't even know where Centralia was, or the man making the call, J. Elroy McCaw. "Les, I know you don't know me, but I've heard you on the air. I own KELA radio, in the twin cities of Centralia-Chehalis, and I'm looking for a young man to break in as assistant sports director. When could you be available to come and talk to me?"

"Well, I'm in Spokane," I managed. (Of course I was in Spokane, he had called me there!) "And I won't be done with my job here until August."

He said the timing was just fine, and we went on to make some arrangements for a visit to Centralia-Chehalis. And on that trip, he offered me the job, effective September 1. I'm not sure what it was he saw in this young sportscaster, but it was something he liked. And to the end of his days, J. Elroy McCaw would be my biggest booster in the field of broadcasting, his path crisscrossing mine periodically, always to my benefit. So I was off to Centralia-Chehalis in my Model A Ford, loaded high with my worldly goods, with my folks along to help me settle in. We checked in at the Lewis & Clark Hotel, also owned by

My Model A Ford got me from Seattle to Spokane and on to Centralia and KELA.

I go on the air with my first sports broadcast in 1941. I am in the white shirt, behind the microphone. Dudley Gaylord (to my left) is the engineer. The Centralia High Tigers are in action.

McCaw, and there was a message to call him at the station. It was a Sunday evening, and he was there. That, too, would prove prophetic. No one worked longer or harder than he did. I was scheduled to start the next morning, but he wanted me to come down to the radio station that night, and I did, arriving at about ten o'clock. He personally gave me the tour and showed me how to operate the board, saying "You'll have a chance to do everything here. You'll do the news, you'll do station breaks, you'll do sports reports, you'll sweep out the place. Ralph Fisher is the sports director, you'll be his assistant, and we'll teach you everything you need to know." Elroy was direct, he was caring, and he knew exactly what he wanted. I did all of the things he said I would (including the part about sweeping), and through that autumn of 1941, I began to learn the real ropes of the business.

Of course, my whole world—everyone's world, really—changed dramatically at the close of the year, on a quiet Sunday morning, December 7, 1941, with Japan's bombing of Pearl Harbor.

Our radio station was taken off the air the next day, as were most West Coast stations, pending an "anticipated" invasion of the Pacific Coast by the Imperial Forces of Japan. I enlisted in the Navy in early 1942. Despite my college education, I was passed over as officer material, due to a physical defect (poor color perception). After completing basic training, I became Les Keiter, Yeoman 3rd Class, U.S. Naval Reserve, and was shipped overseas to Honolulu.

Pearl Harbor was a madhouse, still recovering from the attack six months before. Thousands of us were lined up in front of the administration building to receive our orders, divided among the scores of ships in the harbor: battleships, carriers, submarines, destroyers, tankers, tenders, anything you can imagine, bound for anywhere you can imagine. My assignment took me about thirty yards. I was attached to a commander's office right there in the middle of the Navy yard. It was clerical work, easy and safe and (like most young men of the time) not at all to my liking. I was on the job for about two months when my skipper called me to his desk and said, "I was looking over your records, and I see you're a college graduate. What are you doing as a yeoman? Why don't you have a commission?" I explained to him about the color examination and asked if there was anything he could do about that. He said he'd try.

Six weeks later, a personnel officer called me up. "Is this Yeoman Lester R. Keiter? Report immediately to our office. We have new orders for you, *Ensign.*"

"What?" I asked.

"You've just been promoted, and you're leaving in the next forty-eight hours. Come by and pick up your papers." My skipper had obtained my commission for me and gotten me into the "real" war, or so I thought. Imagine my chagrin when there, in the middle of the Pacific, in the middle of a war zone, I received orders to "proceed on the first available aircraft to Dartmouth College, Hanover, New Hampshire," and after six weeks in officer training to "proceed on the first available transportation to Fort Schuyler, Long Island, New York" for six more weeks of training. So I was headed back to the mainland once again, for at least three months.

After the twelve weeks of training, it looked like I was bound for Solomon Islands, Virginia, to be trained as a skipper on an LST landing craft. That's one of the toughest assignments in the Navy, taking a little boat full of marines into the thick of enemy fire. But another twist of fate occurred: I was assigned instead to Port Hueneme in Southern California to train with the ACORNS. "What the hell are ACORNS?" I wondered, only able to imagine the oak tree variety. As it turned out, ACORNS was an airfield operation unit that came in just behind the Marines and the SEABEEs (Construction Battalions) on a recaptured island. Coincidentally, my brother Buddy had enlisted and been assigned to the SEABEEs, the 11th Special Battalion, but their assignment was going to be in the European theater. I hoped the "Little Guy"—he and the family called me "Big Guy"— would be safe.

The ACORNS' primary mission was to operate airstrips while the ground was still hot from the battle. After training, I was headed to the Russell Islands, just north of Guadalcanal, where the battle was still winding down. It had taken more than six months of training, but by August 1942 I was headed into battle at last. (I would later learn that many of my classmates from Dartmouth and Schuyler did wind up skippering LSTs [Landing Ship Tanks] and LCIs [Landing Craft Infantry] during the murderous invasion of Bougainville, just north of the Russells, and sadly, many of them died.)

Eighteen days out of Port Hueneme (eighteen seasick days for many companions), ACORN 15 arrived in New Caledonia and then moved on to Noumea, HQ, for the Pacific Command under Admiral "Bull" Halsey, whose reputation was just beginning to become known among the public. As I walked along the docks with some shipmates, we came upon an area that was cordoned off and under a Marine guard. The week before an explosion there had killed several Marines and SEABEEs also moving up the slot to the Russell Islands. That was the moment, I think, when the war suddenly became very real to me. When we finally got to the Russells—which were covered with impenetrable jungle—the Harbormaster directed us to our first project, working with the SEABEEs 11th Special Battalion. My friend Billy Lee turned to me and asked, "Isn't that the outfit your brother is with?" Nonsense, I told him, Buddy was sent to Europe; it must be a different part of the 11th Battalion. But that wasn't enough for Billy; he was the curious type.

Billy went up to the harbor master as we were landing and said he had a friend whose brother was sent to Europe with the 11th Special Battalion. The guy smiled and told him, "Yeah, we *were* going to Europe, but after we headed out, they sent us down the East Coast to Panama and into the Pacific. What's your buddy's name?" he asked.

"Keiter. Les Keiter," Billy told him.

"Yeah, I work with his brother. In fact, he's working over there in that tent!" he said, pointing up the dirt road.

Billy ran to me in a frenzy. "Your brother's here, on this island. That guy over there knows him!" he said in a breathless rush. I jogged back to the guy, who recognized the family resemblance. Confirming the story, I asked him not to tell my brother. I wanted to surprise him, and I had a bit of a joke to play on him:

Some years before, when we were both in school, he had asked me the meaning of the word "ironic" for a report he was working on. I explained to him that if I sent him off on a boat headed from Seattle to Japan, and if after the boat left I found out that I had to go there, too, and then took a plane and met his boat as it arrived in Tokyo, that would be *ironic*. Well, I remembered that story and went to surprise Buddy. I encountered him coming toward me on the same road (someone had tipped him off). I grabbed him in a bear hug, and between our laughter and tears asked him, "Now, Buddy, do you understand what *ironic* means?" He did, and we had a great laugh.

BIG GUY AND LITTLE GUY MEET IN THE PACIFIC, read the headline in the Seattle newspaper when the story made its way back home, along with the "ironic" story and pictures in our Navy dress whites. My God, it's amazing the coincidences that can happen in a war. And the happiest of all endings was that both of us would make it home from that terrible conflict. He was soon headed stateside again to work on the V12 program, and I was reassigned to a communications outfit. I bounced around some other Pacific islands before landing for over a year on Peleliu, Palau, where I was finally given something to do that I was good at: running the Palau Armed Forces Radio station.

I was the station manager, and the station was a full-blown operation with a big staff, right out there in the middle of the war. We played records. We did the news. I did sports, and even had my own show. I had a ball. We covered baseball, including an exhibition visit and game with the Navy All-Stars, which included big leaguers Pee Wee Reese, Phil Rizzuto, Johnny Mize, and Joe Grace. This was about as close as any morale-boosting delegation like this got to the action. We still

Big Guy (Les), Little Guy (Buddy), our Navy buddies, and our new Russell Island friends. (Back row) Buddy is third from right, I'm fourth from right.

had some Japanese holding out in some caves up on "Bloody Nose Ridge," just two miles away from the exhibition.

I also broadcast some boxing matches pitting the individual weight champions from various ships, squads, and other outfits against one another. One of the biggest such fights was one of the Marines on the island squaring off for a three-round exhibition match with professional boxer Fred Apostoli, who was then a navy chief specialist. His boxing nickname was "The San Francisco Bell Hop," and he had defeated my boyhood idol, Seattle's own middleweight champion of the world, Freddy Steele. And adding to the occasion, the referee who flew in for the evening was Coast Guard Commodore Gene Tunney, the former heavyweight champion of the world. So there I was, at a ringside card table with my microphone, two world champs, and a Marine who was out for a moment of glory. It was a hell of a moment.

The Marine came out like there was no tomorrow, throwing haymakers at Apostoli, hoping one would get through. The champ, after boxing the Marine off for a round, started to get angry and threw some real punches back, and then the two of them were going at it in earnest, with about five thousand servicemen going crazy watching them, myself included! Finally, mild-mannered Tunney stopped the fight (using his rank to get the word through to the two fighters, now bent on destroying each other), sent the Marine out of the ring, and scolded Apostoli in no small way for brawling with an amateur. And so the fight ended in some disarray, but not before a few minutes of great entertainment. Then, as Tunney got ready to depart, I knew I had a golden opportunity to get an interview with a bona fide sports legend, so I seized it.

My timing wasn't great. Tunney was upset by the turn of events in the ring. He was a gentleman and had walked away from boxing upon his retirement and never looked back. Brawls like this were a part of his own past that he preferred to avoid. So, climbing out of the ring and coming down the steps, the last thing he wanted was an eager, young sportscaster in his path with a microphone. I could see he was angry, and I knew he didn't do interviews, so I hit him with the only weapon I had: "Gene, your shipmates all over the Pacific are listening, could you spare a few minutes to talk to them?"

The gentleman in him prevailed, and he joined me at my rickety little card table for what I knew would be a very brief interview. In fact, I thought I might only get the chance to ask a single question, so I asked *the* question one would ask Gene Tunney: "Gene, could you tell us about your 1927 rematch with Jack Dempsey and the famous 'long count'?" Tunney had won the title from Dempsey in Philadelphia, out-boxing the wilder champion in one of the biggest upsets in ring history. But in the rematch the following year, Dempsey finally connected with Tunney, sending him sprawling against the ropes, and then showering his head and shoulders with more blows. In the confusion over getting Jack Dempsey to a neutral corner before the referee could start his count, Tunney was able to recover his wits, and went on to retain the championship. It was a controversy that was still being talked about more than fifteen years later, when I brought it up to Gene Tunney once more.

I asked just the single question, and without hesitation, Tunney grabbed the microphone and began a monologue. I don't know if it was the truth, or if he had been asked so many times he had a prepared answer, or if he was lying to the whole Pacific theater, but here's how he described the fight—and the famous "long count"—in the quiet, modulated tones of the gentleman he always was:

I wasn't in the ring with a man; I was in there with an animal. Jack Dempsey was the most fearsome puncher that boxing has ever known . . . but I had the superior brain power. I was the intellectual better of Dempsey. I reiterate: he was just an animal. He knew only one thing—when the bell rang, to come out and punch and keep punching until the other man dropped. And that's what he did to every opponent he faced. Until he met me.

When I climbed into the ring I had already defeated him, because I could out-think him. For ten rounds in Philadelphia he couldn't land a glove on me. It was almost cruel to watch. I treated him like a babe in the woods. I won every round, and I was declared the undisputed heavyweight champion. I was ready to announce my retirement, then and there, but everyone screamed for a rematch. So because I am a generous man—and because Jack wanted it so badly—against my better judgment, I agreed to a second fight.

The fight in Chicago was to be my last, and Jack said the same thing, though he did not honor his pledge as I did. The bell rang, and it was like Round Eleven in the previous fight. He couldn't hit Gene Tunney. He was throwing wild punches everywhere, while I tattooed him with my jabs and crossed him with my right. I did all the things a thinking man would do with a wild animal chasing him. I boxed him silly. I closed his eyes so that he could hardly see. Came the seventh round and as I sat there on my stool looking across the ring, I felt sorry for him, because here I had reduced him to helplessness. He was that way, a laggard, a dunce. So I pitied him. And I decided that it was a shame to continue his humiliation—I'll back off these last rounds and let him have a last moment of glory.

Well, he had no understanding of such thinking at all. He continued to chase me like a caged animal, swinging ridiculous punches, and finally I realized it was foolish of me to allow him to hit me, so I backed up against the ropes. Well, Dempsey, completely oblivious of the Marquis of Queensberry Rules—I doubt he knew that a Marquis of Queensberry ever lived—he didn't even know it was a violation to hit a man on the ropes. He just kept punching as I leaned further and further back. And Jack Barry—the referee who *should* have known better—he was in cahoots with Dempsey; he allowed this to continue. So like a thinking man would do I simply sat down, so that the referee would send Dempsey to a neutral corner, and I could get back up and continue the fight. But again, the referee failed in his duty, and allowed the animal to rain blows on me—not that they injured me. Well, I wasn't going to stand up while this nonsense continued, so I waited—it must have been fifteen seconds—for Mr. Barry to come to his senses and take that inhuman beast Dempsey to a neutral corner, which he finally did.

Then I got back up and continued to finish my job, beating Jack Dempsey, and then retired undefeated.

And, with some brief pleasantries, he was on his way. It was a great story, though anyone who had seen the photos in *Ring* magazine of Tunney slumped against the ropes, his eyes rolling and mouth agape, knows that the tale is woefully incomplete. And twenty years later, when both were honored at a Philadelphia banquet that I emceed, I told this version of the fight. When Dempsey took the microphone he glared good-naturedly at Tunney—they had become quite good friends—and snarled, "You've got a lot of nerve telling a cockamamie story like that. It was my mistake—I forgot to go to my neutral corner—but if that stupid referee had been doing his job, I'd have walked away the world champion again!" Tunney just laughed, and Dempsey joined him. The years had taken all the sting away.

Not long after my stint on Palau, I was sent back stateside for reassignment. I stepped off a Mars seaplane on San Francisco's Treasure Island on April 12, 1945. I'll always remember the date, of course, because that was the day President Franklin Delano Roosevelt passed away in Warm Springs, Georgia—the newspaper boys were crying "EXTRA! EXTRA!" in the streets outside my hotel.

When the war ended, it was back to Centralia-Chehalis, and my old job at KELA. Things there hadn't changed much, but I had. I liked my job, but I was yearning for more. And "more" was coming into my life, just around the corner.

Family Affairs

From Centralia to Modesto to Honolulu to San Francisco to New York

WHEN I FIRST MET Lila Jean Hamerslough, she was just a kid. A kid sister, in fact, to one of my fraternity brothers. She was cute, she was still in high school, and as an older, wiser, more mature college man of twenty-one, I never considered the match. Graduation came, the war came, and after a couple of years, I had forgotten all about her.

Back from the war, I was a handsome, strapping, single guy (well, at least one of those was true) pursuing a career. Courtship and marriage were the furthest things from my mind. But there were matchmakers about—that's what mothers are made for, right?—who had other designs. So that's how I found myself being re-introduced to Lila Jean some five years after our first meeting.

She had grown up. Oh baby, had she!

I don't suppose it was love at first sight, but one date led to another, and then another. Looking back now, I think a real

23

turning point was on an outing we took to see the Seattle Rainiers baseball team. Our family dentist had box seats to which we were invited as guests, and settling into our seats, I took out a program, and laboriously began explaining how to keep score of a baseball game—the runs, hits, errors, times-at-bat, RBI, and so on. Of course, like any young man, I had to show off a bit and make the explaining a little more complicated than it probably had to be. But she was a bright girl, and I was certain that with my scoring virtuosity, I could convey at least the basics to her.

She put up with me for about three innings. Then she took the program from me, and simply did it on her own, better than I did. I was somewhat nonplussed, to say the least. Unbeknownst to me, Miss Lila Jean Hamerslough had been the sports editor of her school newspaper. As a girl, she had been named "Outstanding Baseball Fan" by a local paper and listened to Leo Lassen throughout the season. She was one heck of a softball player, too. Lila was as big a sports follower as I ever was or ever would be. We had been dating for some time, and we were close to falling in love, so she didn't want to make a scene about the scoring business. As she says now, "I didn't know if I should play dumb, or show him my smarts." She showed me her smarts then and has continued to ever since!

I proposed to her Easter Sunday morning in 1948, on a dirt road outside of Olympia, Washington. We were married September 9, 1948, in Seattle. My family was there, of course, and her parents Leah and Louie Hamerslough. It was one of the best things—no, *the* best thing—I ever did in my life.

Our honeymoon was a wonderful adventure. Lila had never been east of Olympia, but we solved that in short order. We flew to Chicago (and saw the Cubs), to Cleveland (and saw the Indians), to Niagara (and saw the falls—briefly, before running back to our hotel room), to New York City (and saw every team and Broadway show and big band we could fit into our days there), and Washington, D.C. Somewhere on that trip I told her: "I don't know what the future holds, but I promise you—it will never be dull. And someday, we'll be back in New York . . . to live!" We ended our honeymoon in Los Angeles, and drove up the coast to our first home, an upstairs apartment in Modesto, California.

I had taken a job at an FM station in Modesto, leaving behind some wonderful friends in Centralia-Chehalis—Jack

Wheeler, Harry Hill, Steve Althauser, Bud Housman, George Rowswell, Lyle Nordlund, Walt Lunsford, Cliff Matthews, Sam Forrister, and all the fine folks at KELA radio. When I told Lila that Modesto was where our married life would begin, her first reaction was "Where the heck is Modesto?" Fortunately for me, the city was only ninety minutes away from the shopping and culture of San Francisco, otherwise I don't know if Lila would ever have forgiven me. It would be the only career decision I ever made without her.

In fact, Modesto was a charming town (now it's a thriving city), and a fairly good career move for me. The station, KBEE-FM, was just going on the air as part of the Eleanor McClatchey radio empire. Few folks had FM receivers at the time, but Mrs. McClatchey had guessed—correctly—that it would be the medium of the future. Her strategy to get people to buy FM radios was to dominate the sports broadcasts in the area. I would be broadcasting home games live and re-create the away games of the Modesto Bees, the Class-A California State League team owned by the St. Louis Browns. The now-defunct Browns were one of the closest big league teams to California or any of the West Coast cities. This was a decade before the Giants and Dodgers moved from New York. So the California State League was the biggest baseball attraction in town. I also broadcast the live home games of the nearby Stockton team, and re-creations of the rest of the league. I also covered all the other local sports. Lila and I arrived in October, I carried her over the threshold, and the football season started.

It turned out we were in Modesto for just four or five months. In the middle of the basketball season, I received a telegram from Honolulu and J. Elroy McCaw, my former KELA Radio employer and sometime mentor: "WONDERFUL OPPORTUNITY FOR YOU HERE, IF INTERESTED." We sent back: "ALWAYS INTERESTED. SEND DETAILS."

When he did, we went.

We packed up our bags and flew to Hawaii on British Commonwealth Pacific Airlines, over ten hours in transit. Lila thought it was the end of the world. As we sighted the Islands, I was reminded of the thoughts that passed through my mind during my military flight away from Hawaii, half a decade before: "I never want to see this god-forsaken rock again." Looking through the window of the BCPA airliner, I knew I had been wrong. Hawaii was magnificent.

We found a little home on Pau Street in Waikiki, and I went to work. The job for Elroy was as sports director for KPOA-AM radio (television was still a couple of years away), and it was in a little studio on Beretania Street where I began by re-creating baseball on a full-time basis: two games a day, seven days a week—major league games in the afternoon, San Francisco Seals games in the evening. Seals owner Paul Fagan lived in Hana, Maui—his family still does—and he had brought Don Klein to Hawaii as my predecessor. Frank Valenti, now owner of Hawaii's largest advertising agency, joined me later to help with the games. Lila was my statistician. She kept a huge book filled with the scores and statistics from the eight Pacific Coast League teams, as well as the National and American leagues. It still makes me wince to think of that awful scorekeeping lesson I had tried to give her. She was great, a real pro. I had a fresh scorebook every day and every night on every player. She held the job throughout our two years in Honolulu and during her first pregnancy. As she says now, she kept track of the statistics until she decided to make a few of her own.

We adored Hawaii. We went to the beach early every day. When time permitted, we would go to movies at the wonderful

A reunion of the KPOA sports broadcast team of 1949 and 1950. We re-created fourteen baseball games a week. (L–R) Carlos Rivas, Frank Valenti, and me.

Waikiki Theatre—seventy-five cents a ticket, reserved seats. We went to the Hawaiian shows at the hotels—there weren't nearly so many then as now. We shopped at Everybody's Market in Kapahulu. We played canasta for hours with our neighbors, the Coppels. It was like a perpetual vacation. A little after a year, Lila became pregnant with our first child. We were settling in for a bit of a stay.

But it wasn't to be. In the early fall of 1950, Elroy offered me a position in San Francisco as sports director at KYA radio. The West Coast was in the midst of a post-war boom, and the Bay Area was quickly becoming a metropolis. It was a big move up for me career-wise, and after serious discussion, we decided to take it. It was a sorrowful goodbye. In our twenty months in Hawaii, we had made some very close friends, both in and out of the broadcasting and sports community. We were honored with a big farewell luncheon at the Quarterback Club, and many tears were shed.

Lila was eight months pregnant, and her doctor checked her over carefully before giving a thumbs up for the ten-hour trip back to San Francisco. We loaded our bags, boarded the plane, and promised ourselves we'd be back. It would be twenty years and five kids later, but it was a promise we would keep.

We were greeted in San Francisco by my folks, who had since moved there to open a new tobacco store, and by Lila's brother Herb, who lived there. We set up yet another household—our third in as many years—and I went to work again, picking up mid-season for college football: Stanford, California, San Jose State, Santa Clara, St. Mary's, and College of the Pacific. We were still settling in, with help from Lila's folks who were visiting from Seattle, when things were somewhat unsettled by the arrival on November 10, 1950, of Richard Allan Keiter—"Ricky" for the rest of his life. Now the Keiters were three. Lila proved to be as adept a mother as a scorekeeper, and over time I learned how to do my part.

San Francisco wasn't a big league town yet, but they took their sports seriously, and station manager Jock Fearnhead—also out of Honolulu—and I were determined to deliver as much action as we could lay our hands on. This was in addition to the college football, basketball, and other sports we currently broadcast, sponsored by the big local school booster, Tidewater Associated Oil. We signed up with the Liberty Network, which specialized in baseball re-creations. The Liberty Network was

I am interviewing the great heavyweight champion Joe Louis.

the brainchild of Gordon McClendon, an announcer who called himself "The Old Scotsman" (though in fact, he was no older than I was) and his father B. R. McClendon, who financed the operation (the joke at the time was that the "B. R." stood for "Bank Roll"). The Liberty Network produced some great announcers, including Lindsey Nelson and Jerry Doggett, Vin Scully's longtime partner.

After a season of Liberty baseball, we began doing major league re-creations on our own. And as had happened in Honolulu, and would happen again in the future, it was baseball re-creations that would make my reputation in the Bay Area. A re-creation is just what it sounds like: taking the statistics of a game and re-creating the action as if it were live, something that could happen only on radio. McCaw's methods for getting the game statistics—he once hired a spotter to phone the details of Dodgers' games from a tree overlooking Brooklyn's Ebbets Field—were in a gray legal area, and would eventually lead to charges of game "piracy," but my responsiblity was not to reason why, mine was but to broadcast daily from the Fairmont Hotel.

Time passed quickly in San Francisco. Lila became pregnant once more, and soon we were preparing for the arrival of another Keiter. By the fall of 1952, Lila was in full bloom, and her parents were visiting for the Thanksgiving holidays. In fact it was her mother, not Lila, who first noticed that Lila's labor had begun, and insisted we go to the hospital. Lila thought it was ridiculous, but consented. We called Dr. Louie Goldstein, who had delivered Ricky, and headed to the hospital. On arrival, an earthquake shook the place. I should have recognized it as an omen.

Lila, despite her protests over *not* being in labor, was in fact, minutes away from delivery. The doctor rushed her out, leaving me and my father in the waiting room. So we waited— that's what fathers did in those days. But soon, I noticed a lot of commotion down the corridor. Then a voice (it sounded like Lila's) shouted something (it sounded like "Twins?!"). I turned to my dad and relayed, "I heard 'twins.' " Jake replied in a booming voice that could be heard up and down the halls: "TWINS? JESUS CHRIST! NO! IT CAN'T BE!"

Yes, it was. A boy and a girl, Martin Bruce and Barbara Ruth Keiter. Now we were five. They had been lying on top of each other in such a way that only one heartbeat could be picked up. It was a surprise to everyone. Poor Lila. When they wheeled her gurney past me in the corridor, she said weakly, "I hope you're not mad at me, honey, there are *two* of them."

I called the two mothers back at the house. Lila's mother answered and excitedly asked, "Is it a boy or a girl?"

"Yes," I told her. She repeated her question, and I the answer. She told Dolly I had gone soft in the head and handed her the phone.

"Well, what is it son, a girl or a boy?" my mother asked.

"Yes," I told her. And she promptly asked to talk to the doctor, who finally explained it all, somewhat to his own chagrin.

"But there are no twins in our family!" Dolly protested.

"There are now," said Dr. Louie. Mother, son, and daughter were all healthy, and soon we were back home together.

My dad's first visit caused quite a stir, when he came through the door beaming. "Where are those new twins of mine?" he called, pushing past Ricky to get to the bedroom. Ricky, who worshiped the ground his grandfather walked on, was devastated. But later, when we discovered the slight he had inadvertently suffered, we took him aside and told him how much help his new siblings were going to need from their big brother. "Me?" he asked. We nodded. With his next visit to the nursery, Ricky adopted the new arrivals into his little heart.

After three years in the Bay Area, J. Elroy McCaw was hatching a new scheme, and it would take us to a place where we always knew we would go. He and partner Jack Keating had purchased another radio station, and with a single phone call over a weekend, he once again turned our lives upside down.

"Be in New York a week from Monday. You're the new sports director at WINS Radio in Manhattan," he told us. In just ten days, we had to settle the affairs of a home and a car, move three children, two of whom were still infants, and do whatever else it takes to move from one end of the country to the other. We were told not to worry; Elroy would take care of everything on the New York end.

Well, to a point. On arrival, after an overnight plane journey from San Francisco—one baby in Lila's arms for twelve hours, one baby in mine—we were met by a WINS staffer who took us to a place they had rented for our first few weeks in New York. The brochure he showed us looked fine. The room, unfortunately, didn't match the brochure. It was a dive. Lila and I would have been okay, but with the kids? . . . At least the crib sheets were clean, so we put the twins down with their bottles, and Lila delivered a single command. "Les, do something." I

Les' Enthusiasm is Catching

My favorite hyperthyroidal broadcaster used to be Les Keiter, who re-created baseball locally before moving to New York and louder things. Les is heard here occasionally on radio for heavyweight championship fights. He is bombastic, bloody and thorough. Once, it is said, the two men in the ring were so fascinated they stopped fighting and leaned over the ring ropes to hear how they were doing.

San Francisco Examiner, March 19, 1964, from Art Rosenbaum's "Sporting Green"

called frantically. Nothing was available. I suppose in this respect, New York City has changed little in four decades. Eventually, I booked us a room—a suite in fact—at the Mayflower Hotel on Columbus Circle, overlooking Central Park. We called a cab and moved that same day. Talk about going from famine to feast! It was ridiculous. Money never disappeared so fast, but it was all we could do until we were settled. We immediately started looking for a real home.

Fortunately, our friends from Honolulu, the Coppels, had family in New York, and they became our guides and guardians for our first few weeks, directing us in shopping, medical care, you-name-it. We looked everywhere, from New Jersey to Connecticut to Westchester. Eventually, we settled rather unenthusiastically for a new apartment building in Westchester, but at the last minute looked at a house in Manhasset, on Long Island. We took it for the incredibly high rent of two hundred fifty dollars a month, and Long Island became our home for the next ten years. We later bought a house nearby and still later bought one in neighboring Port Washington. New York was now the official base of Keiter operations.

Three years later, the family would grow once more. Of course, Lila's first question on learning of her pregnancy was, "Could it be twins again?"

Her obstetrician, Dr. Arnold Fenton, assured her repeatedly throughout the next eight months that it would not be so. He would stake his reputation on it.

So it would be with no little shock, when on February 4, 1958, he walked from the delivery room to the waiting room to tell me, "Les, they're just fine. All three of them."

I reeled. "TRIPLETS?!" No, it was only twins, little girls as tiny as could be, but healthy enough for their size. It would be some weeks before even one of them could come home, and they were still little bitty things until they were a couple of months old. Cindy Marlene and Jodi Sue Keiter were the names chosen after some deliberation. After all, we were only expecting one. Lila, of course, would never let Dr. Fenton hear the end of it. Two sets of twins, two doctors, and not a word of advance warning. It was as much as the medical profession could ask of any mother.

By this time, I was doing basketball for the New York Knicks. The team, and their wives, had been following the pregnancy along with Lila and me. I walked into Madison Square

Now we are seven! (L–R) Twin Jodi being held by Ricky, twin Cindy being held by twin Marty, and twin Barbara.

Garden after leaving the hospital, arriving about halfway through the first game of a doubleheader. As I headed up to the booth, I was spotted by one of the players, Larry Friend, who shouted across the arena, "ANY NEWS?" I answered by simply holding up two fingers. He relayed the news to the team, and they went wild. Good friends, all of them.

Now, we were seven. And that would fill up the Keiter team roster until the next generation. But this is getting a little ahead of the story. First I had to get the job going in the Big Apple. I was ready.

The New Kid in New York

And how impressed
Casey Stengel was with me

NEW YORK CITY, 1953. This was what it was all about.

All those years in Seattle, Modesto, Centralia-Chehalis, Honolulu, and even San Francisco were preparatory; New York was the Dream Come True. New York is affectionately called the Big Apple, and for a newcomer like me, no description could have been more apt. The city was jumping. Everything was happening . . . and I was a small part of it!

I remember my first luncheon meeting of the Sports Broadcasters Association. My food sat untouched as I stared at who was sitting at the tables. I was surrounded by gods—Mel Allen, Red Barber, Russ Hodges, Curt Gowdy, Don Dunphy, and dozens like them—the people that this young rookie saw (and still sees) as the giants of the sports broadcasting industry. And I was among them, hobnobbing and hearing those wonderful voices address me by name. I was star-struck and starry-eyed.

Throughout the 1950s, WINS Radio was the top sports station in New York—and I was its sports director.

I wasn't the only Keiter that was knocked out by the sports stars that shone in the big city. My father and mother came for a visit shortly after we arrived. Dad was a great sports fan, so I took him to a *Sports Illustrated* awards luncheon where, as sports director of WINS, I was one of the presenters. We checked into the VIP room before the luncheon began, and I saw a trio of people I had had the pleasure of meeting in my first few months on the job. "Dad, I'd like you to say hello to some friends of mine," I said as they approached us. "I'd like you to meet Mrs. Babe Ruth, Mrs. Lou Gehrig, and Jack Dempsey."

"Nice to see you again, Les," said Dempsey as he extended his hand to my unbelieving father. I had just done an interview with Jack at his restaurant a few weeks before. "I hope you enjoy your stay in New York, Mr. Keiter." Dad nearly fainted. As we walked away, he asked in a shaky voice, "My God, do you know who those people are?" I knew. And I knew it could only happen in New York.

We were still in the process of looking for a permanent home when station owner J. Elroy McCaw phoned. "How are things going, Les?"

What a nice guy, checking up on his newest employee. "Fine, we're house hunting on Long Island this weekend."

"No, you're not. You will be flying to St. Petersburg, Florida. Monday you'll be doing your first broadcast from the New York Yankees training camp."

"But—" I began.

"Once the regular season begins you'll be doing the Yankees pre-game show every night. This will introduce you to the fans and the sponsors."

Well, I could argue all I wanted about my responsibilities to my family, but when the magic word "sponsors" came into play, I knew I had to give it up. Lila, irritated but understanding, helped me pack my bags. (Later that spring we found a home on Long Island with a beautiful yard, a school across the street, and lots of children in the neighborhood. It helped considerably in apologizing to the family for my rather rude and sudden departure.) I flew to Florida, leaving the late winter of the North for the early spring of the Southeast.

Spring training was the time of year all of baseball was optimistic. The owners, managers, coaches, and players were all declaring that this was going to be their year! Spring training was one of the most enjoyable experiences my family ever had. In the 1950s most of the teams trained in Florida. The Yankees and the St. Louis Cardinals trained in St. Petersburg, sharing Al Lang Field. The Cincinnati Reds were nearby in Tampa, the Philadelphia Phillies in Clearwater, the Brooklyn Dodgers at Vero Beach, and Palm Beach was home for the Milwaukee Braves. The remaining teams were sprinkled throughout the state. To get our stories, we'd shuttle between the training camps in a rented Chevy—Yankees broadcasters Red Barber, Mel Allen and Les Keiter, singing at the top of our lungs as we cruised the blacktop highways. Pretty frightening image, eh?

Things were a little more casual then, not the big business atmosphere of recent years. The wives and kids of all the players came down, and at the end of practice most of the players would gather their families and head for the beach. There was a handful of restaurants in Tampa and Clearwater Beach where anyone could walk in and find the best of the baseball world in a single room: players, coaches, managers, even a rookie announcer or two. It was a great time of year for all of us.

The 1950s were Golden Years for the Yankees, who have always seemed to create new eras of Golden Years every decade or so. Yogi Berra was the catcher, famous for his wonderful way of murdering the English language. ("It ain't over 'til it's over," and "Thank you all for making this day necessary.") He earned his Hall of Fame status as one of the greatest hitters and catchers of all time, and today he's still in the game in the front office in Houston. At first base was Joe Collins, and later, the great clutch hitter Moose Skowron, both consummate Yankees. The 1950s Yankees had several second basemen: Billy Martin, Gil McDougald, and later, Bobby Richardson. A utility infielder who played a lot of second base was Jerry Coleman, now the voice of the San Diego Padres. Jerry was not a great hitter, but one of the smoothest fielders of that era. Phil "Scooter" Rizzuto was at short, and why he isn't yet a Hall of Famer is a mystery to many, including me. At third was Gil McDougald (later he played second base and shortstop), who had the misfortune of hitting the line drive that ultimately took Cleveland pitcher Herb Score out of baseball. Gene Woodling was in left field, and Hank Bauer was in right field. And in center field was Mickey Mantle, the big farm kid from Commerce, Oklahoma, who took over center field for Joe DiMaggio and became the symbol of the Yankees. Mantle could run, he could field, he could throw, and baby, could he hit, and from either side of the plate, too! An out-of-the-park homer at Griffith Stadium in Washington, D.C., was once measured at 565 feet! The 1950s Yankees pitching staff also reads like a Who's Who of Baseball: Whitey Ford, Johnny Sain, Bob Turley, Don Larsen, and Johnny Kucks.

The Yankees have had their share of colorful characters over the years. One who kept popping up in Yankees circles until his untimely death in 1989 was Billy Martin. Billy the Kid became the premier second baseman of the 1950s and 1960s by playing with fierce determination and tenacity. Manager Casey Stengel always said Martin "couldn't catch, couldn't throw, and couldn't hit . . . but he would just *beat* you." I recall one memorable World Series game at Ebbets Field in Brooklyn. A short pop fly was lifted between the third baseline and the pitcher's mound, and it looked as if no Yankee was going to go after it. The third baseman stayed to cover third, the catcher stayed at home, and the pitcher just stood there watching the ball begin to drop. If the ball was not caught, the Dodgers would have won the game. Martin streaked over *from second base*—he lost his cap running for it—and he made the catch, saving the

Casey Stengel may have preferred a new pitcher over a new sportscaster, but he was always available for an interview.

game for the Yankees! What a battler! Of course, his gift for finding a fight is legendary—just ask George Steinbrenner. As a manager, Billy Martin still had that way of "just beating you"—he made winners out of Detroit, New York (on several occasions), Minnesota, Oakland and Texas. He always wound up getting fired, but he knew how to win. But this was all in the future. Back in the 1950s, he was "Casey's Boy."

And there, of course, was another legend, Casey Stengel, Yankees manager par excellence. My very first day in spring training, Mel Allen presented me to Mr. Stengel (who I believe must have been born grizzled—it's impossible to imagine him any other way!) "Casey," said Mel, "I'd like you to meet Les Keiter. He's our new announcer for the Yankees broadcasts." Casey turned away from the batting cage, looked me up and down once, and growled, "Announcer? I don't need any more announcers! I need a pitcher!" and then turned back to work. I was certain that my broadcasting career had just ended, that Allen would put me on the next bus back to San Francisco. But for Stengel it was simply standard operating procedure. I would interview him often in the following weeks (and years), and while I can't say he ever mellowed, the interviews certainly ceased being as traumatic as that initial encounter.

On the surface, early spring training appears very languid and relaxed, but underneath there is an incredibly competitive atmosphere. Unlike the team competition of the baseball season itself, the battle at training camp is an individual one. The lack of agents, personal managers, and million-dollar contracts didn't make any difference—then, as now, the athletes were fighting for their careers. Spring training determines whether the player is going to be traveling by plane (big leagues) or by bus (minor leagues), and spending his meal allowance in fancy restaurants or in greasy spoons. For the rookie, this is the chance to make the big club; for the veterans, a hope to keep the big-league salary and prestige for one more season. The established stars—the Mantles, Berras, and Fords—had it a little easier. They were told to set their own pace, build themselves up gradually, shed the winter fat, and be ready on opening day. But even for the established stars it was difficult to ignore the five fellows fighting for *their* jobs. And everyone worried about getting injured.

Perhaps the biggest difference for the players between the 1950s and today is the level of conditioning. Many of the older-era players did little or no off-season conditioning. Spring training was used to get back into playing shape. Today the professional athlete shows up in camp already in shape. Spring training is more for getting the touch back on that curve ball or slider, sharpening the batting eye or improving defensive skills, not shedding the winter fat. There is just too much money today for the professional athlete to allow any other player any advantage.

Every summer for seven years, from 1953 to 1960, I did the Yankees pre-game show, then turned the microphone over to the broadcast team of Mel Allen and Jim Woods. In later years I introduced the play-by-play duo of Mel Allen and Red Barber. Every winter would end with a trip south to Florida. Being part of the Yankees family is one of the all-time personal highlights of my career, and when I say "family," I really mean it. Lila and the kids would come down, too. We've got albums full of snapshots of son Ricky with Mickey Mantle, Jerry Coleman, Billy Hunter, Yogi Berra, and Phil Rizzuto—the players adopted him, and he in turn was a dedicated Yankees fan.

During my time with the Yankees, it seemed as if every World Series would pit the Yankees against the Brooklyn Dodgers. The papers seemed to write about a subway series every fall. New York and baseball just went together. Watching the Yankees was a delight for Lila and me. I must admit we are a tad more partial to the baseball diamond than to any other playing field. Perhaps the most powerful images evoked by the three New York teams were their men in center field: Mickey Mantle in Yankee Stadium, Dodger Duke Snider over at Ebbets Field, and the delightful Willie Mays playing for the Giants at the Polo Grounds. Three great teams, three great parks, three great ballplayers.

Our old Hawaii friend, H. G. "Jock" Fearnhead, joined WINS as general manager a few months after I arrived. We both wanted another sports plum to follow up the summer of live Yankees broadcasts and re-created Giants baseball. We decided that if WINS was to be considered the major sports station in New York, it needed the New York Giants football broadcasts. So we waited for their radio contract to expire and went after the rights with a vengeance and a very impressive financial package. WMGM Radio had covered the Giants games for years and expected to do so for years to come, so it was quite a coup when WINS acquired the broadcasting rights agreement from co-

Every young baseball player's dream—Ricky with Mickey Mantle and Yogi Berra.

The legendary Red Barber and me during a Yankees broadcast.

owners Jack and Wellington Mara. Broadcasting the Giants football would be my first opportunity to do live play-by-play in the Big Apple. When it came time to select a color man, I wanted to team up with veteran announcer Marty Glickman. Marty was a former New York University and 1936 Olympic track star and was the Voice of the Giants for WMGM. I thought it would be great to have the continuity of his presence on our broadcasts. It would also be a personal thrill to work with someone of his stature. Marty was a true Mr. Big in New York sports circles, so looking back I guess I was a little naive when I called him—relative rookie to established sportscaster—and offered him a job with me to continue with Giants football.

"Hey, wait a minute," was his response, "Marty Glickman doesn't do color with anybody. Either I'm Number One, or I'm not on the broadcast."

Mr. Stupid Nice Guy that I was, I assumed he misunderstood, so I started to explain the offer again.

"You apparently didn't hear me," he bellowed, "Marty Glickman doesn't do color with anybody." End of conversation. So much for being a nice guy. It was one of my first encounters with big league sportscasting egos, though certainly not my last. I covered the 1953 season for the Giants and continued for eight seasons more, through the fall of 1961, sharing the booth with John Condon, Jim Gordon, Tommy Henrich, and others.

The Giants were loaded with fabulous personnel. Jim Lee Howell was the coach from 1954 to 1960. The Giants were a winning operation from the front office to the playing field. Their defense, now legendary, was incredible: linebacker Sam Huff;

Are the Giants' Runners Really that Slow?

Now that Les Keiter has brought some of his re-creating brilliance to pro football, one can understand why he finds mere facts too dull to deal with after educating his followers to expect more from him than a strictly factual recital of what's taking place on the field. Sometimes this technique doesn't adapt itself readily to football.

For instance, when Alex Webster reached the five-yard line on a 17-yard touchdown run, Les, keying himself up to C above Middle C, screamed in a rapid, hysterical crescendo "he's at the five; he's at the four; he's at the three; he's at the two; he's at the one; it's a touchdown for the Giants!"

It took Les about six seconds to describe five yards of this touchdown journey. There are halfbacks who, in full football regalia, could run half the length of the field in that time, so I take it that in those last five yards, Alex must have inched his way through the defense do-ing the Charleston alternating with a lateral shuffle off to Buffalo at every yard to throw the enemy off balance.

I'm not aiming to undermine the Giants' box of-fice when I say that listening to Les Keiter's version of the game is better than seeing the original. I am merely stating a fact which will be borne out by most of his 10,000,000 followers.

New York Mirror, October 1958,
from Dan Parker's column

lineman Dick Modzelewski, who would go on to coach in the
NFL; the two Roosevelts, Rosey Grier and Roosevelt Brown;
Andy Robustelli; Jim Katcavage; Don Chandler; and in the defensive backfield was Tom Landry, destined to be the longtime
coach of the Dallas Cowboys. On offense, Charley Conerly was
the quarterback, later succeeded by Y. A. Tittle. The running
backs were Frank Gifford and Kyle Rote. At fullback was Alex
Webster, a future Giants coach whose record for career yardage
was only recently challenged. What a lineup! With that kind of
talent you just can't help but play great football.

Jim Lee Howell was a tall, white-haired, no-nonsense kind
of coach who simply knew how to win. He surrounded himself
with a first-rate staff. One staff member was a line coach who
today is revered as the pre-eminent pro coach of all time, Vince
Lombardi. Lombardi had been one of the "Seven Blocks of
Granite" when he played at Fordham University and was later a
coach at Army. In the early 1950s he was continuing to build
his reputation with the Giants, and looking back, I feel fortunate
that I had the chance to spend so much time with him *before*
the years of fame and glory in Green Bay, Wisconsin. I spent
many a Monday Giants' luncheon with him, talking about the
Giants, the NFL, football, New York, philosophy, or whatever
was on our minds. He was not only interested in football. He
was interested in what made us the complex human beings that
we are. He was hard-nosed and tough-talking, but underneath
he was a very warm human being. And boy, could he do his
job! You just knew this guy wasn't going to be an assistant
coach forever, that some special showcase awaited him. I don't
think anyone could have predicted the near-sainthood he
achieved, but clearly, there was some kind of special greatness
awaiting him.

This was all pre-Super Bowl, of course, but there was a
division championship game. The team dominated the 1950s,
finishing at or near the top every year. The Giants' two most
likely opponents in the championship game were each led by
superstars of the era: Jim Brown and the Cleveland Browns and
young Johnny Unitas with the Baltimore Colts. No wonder the
Giants were a great defensive team: you *had* to be to stop those
two players!

WINS lost the Giants contract to WCBS after six seasons.
The acquisition of the Giants broadcast rights was spearheaded
by WCBS' Jimmy Dolan, a major NFL figure from way back.

I'll never forget that day he called to say that unfortunately the Giants wouldn't be needing my play-by-play services for the upcoming NFL season. "I'm sorry Les, but you're simply too widely identified as the sports director of WINS. I respect your talent and your years with the club, but WCBS has to have their own team on the air."

This was certainly understandable, and such changes are a fact of life in broadcasting. I appreciated the personal call. Secrets lasting as long as they do in this business, it was only a matter of minutes before the phone calls of questions and condolences began coming in from friends, acquaintances, and strangers. About an hour later I answered the call from someone whose loud, gruff voice was immediately recognizable.

"Hello, Les? This is Bert Bell." Bert was the commissioner of the NFL. He was calling long-distance from the league's home office in Philadelphia. "Les, what's this crap"—he actually used a stronger word—"that you're not going to be doing the Giants this fall?"

"Well, Bert," I began to explain, "the contract has been acquired by WCBS Radio and—"

"Who the hell cares what station it's on?" he interrupted. "I don't give a fig"—again stronger language (Bert was a master of vulgarities)—"I don't give a fig about stations. You are a part of the NFL, you are one of *our* announcers, and so help me as Commissioner of the National Football League, Les Keiter is *the* voice of the New York Giants!"

Of course it was a personal thrill to hear such words from a man of such power and position, but I had to tell him, "Bert, your saying it and my hearing it can't make it so. WCBS has a contract that—"

"Who's the guy over there?" he demanded.

"Jimmy Dolan."

"You'll hear from me!" and he hung up.

It wasn't forty minutes later that the phone rang again. It was Jimmy Dolan.

"Les, I want you to know how very sorry I am about my previous call. I want you to know that we'd be delighted to have you continue as the play-by-play man for the Giants. Could you meet me tomorrow for lunch so we can work out a contract?" It was that clean and simple. (Jimmy and I went on to become good friends, sharing rides in from Long Island to the stadium and working together on the games. Jimmy is one of

the best producers I ever had the pleasure of sharing a broadcast booth with—a true professional.)

I did feel that a thank you call to Bert was in order, but
when I phoned he wouldn't hear of it. "You don't have to thank
me! You're our man in New York and nobody's going to tell
me different! It's done!" And when I saw him in Philadelphia a
few months later, he winked and said simply, "Well, we pulled
that one off, didn't we kid?!" What a great guy! He passed away
the next year, suffering a heart attack while watching his beloved NFL at an Eagles game, and he was greatly mourned and
missed by many—certainly by this young sportscaster, who owed
him at least one enormous debt.

With the Yankees and the Giants football wrapped up, we
set our sights on New York's major indoor sports venue: Madison Square Garden. Jock Fearnhead gave me the thumbs up to
open a dialogue with Ned Irish, president of the Garden, and
Fred Podesta, Irish's assistant. Madison Square Garden was the
home of both the NBA Knickerbockers and the NHL Rangers,
and though WINS was after both, we had a particular interest
in securing the basketball rights. As with the Giants, the Knicks
had to that point been broadcasting with WMGM and my fellow
"voice" Marty Glickman.

Glickman, in fact, was so much a part of basketball at the
Garden it could be heard in his play-by-play lingo. Anyone who
has been to a Knicks home game knows about the soft drink
called Nedick's, a popular East Coast orange drink. Nedick's
was a major radio sponsor for the games. And whenever a
Knicks player made an incredible shot, Marty would announce
to his audience, "Good! Like Nedick's!" In time the phrase
became synonymous with Madison Square Garden, the Knicks,
and Marty Glickman.

But once again, after lengthy negotiations, WINS secured
the broadcast rights for the upcoming Knicks season.

Vince Boryla was the coach in the early 1950s. He may
be the only player to earn All-American honors at two different
universities, first at Denver and then at Notre Dame. He later
achieved fame as a Knicks player and then went on to become
their head coach. The Knicks' star players included Richie
Guerin, Carl Sobie, Dick McGuire, and Carl Braun. Ray Felix
was the seven-foot center (who would delight my family by
signing his autograph on a ten-foot-high ceiling beam in our
living room). There was Charlie Tyra; Guy Sparrow from De-

troit; the golden boy from Santa Clara, Ken Sears; Nat "Sweetwater" Clifton; and one of the greatest players in UCLA history, Willie Naulls. Boryla's assistant was "Fuzzy" Levane, who later replaced Boryla as head coach.

Despite such great talent, the 1950s were struggling years for the Knicks. There was stiff competition in the league, particularly from the perennial champion Boston Celtics. Coach Red

The Not-So-Instant Replay

The Case of the Cuckoo Clock was placed on NBA president Maurice Podoloff's docket yesterday when Fred Podesta, Knicks' business manager, forwarded a letter of protest to the league office along with a $250 forfeit check.

It all started in Cincinnati Wednesday night in the closing minutes of a contest won by the Royals, 110–108. With the score 106–104 in favor of Cincinnati, Carl Braun was about to take a foul shot with the clock showing 2:25 to play. But the timer called referees Norm Drucker and Arnie Heft over to the table and told them the clock wasn't functioning properly.

The timer said it had jumped from 2:00 to 2:59 instead of 1:59 and read, when time was called, an erroneous 2:25. He claimed the correct amount of time to play should read 1:25.

Both refs told him to correct the error and that brought a howl from the Knicks. Knicks coach, Fuzzy Levane, said he had running sheets of both New York and Cincinnati newspapermen to point to as well as Les Keiter's taped version of the game.

The running score sheet, kept by the Royal's staff, also showed the time that Braun stepped to the foul line at 2:25. It was later typed over to read 1:25 to conform with the referees' decision.

All of this data as well as Keiter's tape recording will be turned over to Podoloff as evidence.

New York Daily News, December 5, 1958

Auerbach had a team filled with all-stars: Bob Brannum, Bill Sharman, Bob Cousy, Bill Russell, Sam Jones, K. C. Jones, Tom Heinsohn, and Jim Luscotoff. Other great players the Knicks faced included Bob Pettit and Cliff Hagen at St. Louis; Wilt Chamberlain with the Philadelphia Warriors; the Minneapolis Lakers' George Mikan, Jim Pollard, and Slater Martin; and the Syracuse Nationals' Hal Gregg, Larry Costello, and Dolph Schayes, whose son, Danny, is now playing in the NBA.

There was another member of the Knicks organization who has since become very well known to NBA fans. The team ball boy, who took care of towels and jackets and the like, was a bright kid who later attended Syracuse University. In fact, on Knicks road games in Syracuse, I used him as my scorekeeper. He was determined to become a professional sportscaster, and even at that young age you could see he would be good. His name was Marv Albert, and he's still broadcasting the Knicks after two decades of play-by-play, as well as earning well-deserved success in many other areas of national sports broadcasting.

My years with the Knicks also led to the broadcast of the biggest fight of my career—at least when judged by the number of participants involved! The Knicks were playing the Warriors in Philadelphia's Convention Hall, where the spectators' seats came right up to courtside. It was a very physical game with lots of bumping, elbowing, and pushing. Tempers flared throughout the first three quarters, but the referees were just able to keep the game under control. Midway through the fourth quarter, Woody Sauldsberry of the Warriors took offense at an elbow thrown by Richie Guerin. Sauldsberry charged Guerin and wrestled him all the way up into the fourth or fifth row! Philadelphia fans, being the great sports enthusiasts that they are, decided to join in the fray. Some quick-thinking fans wrapped Guerin up in their overcoats and began swinging away! The rest of the Knicks players in the game rushed into the stands to help Guerin. The Warriors followed. Then everybody on both benches joined the fray, and I mean *everybody*—coaches, players, ball boys, the works! In seconds, a good portion of the crowd was involved too, while I—out of a sense of journalistic responsibility, of course—took cover under my table and kept talking! I described for the listening audience the non-stop action of chairs flying, players fighting players, players fighting fans, fans fighting fans, officials pulling at heaps of players, and bloodied noses.

Les Leaves Them in Stitches

In the recorded history of the middleweight boxing division the Joey Giardello–Hurricane Carter bout will not rank with the first Graziano–Zale fight; nor the second; nor the third. The best thing about it was Les Keiter, who turned in another of his wonderful re-creations. You remember Les; he used to do those exciting Giants baseball games that were played in Frisco the first year Willie Mays moved out there. Keiter watched the Giants play on a flat Western Union tape, in a New York booth, 3,000 miles away. He was magnificent; what imagination!

Keiter has lost none of his imagination. He sat at ringside in Philly on Monday night and conjured up a pretty good fight. The show came on right after Jonathan Winters, and it's a good thing for Winters it wasn't full network or he would have been slaughtered in the ratings. Keiter was much funnier. He had the select studio audience in stitches throughout the fight.

Lines like, "The champion just winked in our direction," or "Carter is smiling more than before. Does he know something?" and "There's a right to the body by Giardello and now Carter is bleeding from the nose," followed by a clarification, "It's quite possible I've misread that blood and that it's just Carter's Fu Manchu mustache dripping down!"

Keiter had an assistant, a color man, who provided probing analyses between rounds. His name was Hal Freeman yet one time was called Hal Newman by Les. Hal got even for this indignity later in the fight when he handed the microphone back to Keiter with, "Take it away, Les Carter."

But Keiter led Freeman on points all the way. Freeman, a countering commentator, finished fast, and had his best flurry just before the 15th. It was then, after 14 rounds, that Hal weighed things carefully and announced: "Those who predicted an early knockout are definitely wrong."

New York Daily News, December 16, 1964,
from Dick Young's column

It must have gone on for ten full minutes until order was finally restored. Following the expected ejections, the somewhat subdued teams finished the game. The final chapter of the story wasn't played out until after the game. Both teams had to ride from Philadelphia to New York for the next night's doubleheader . . . on the same bus! The trip was made in dead silence. If the tension hadn't been so thick, I think I would have laughed out loud.

Our Madison Square Garden relationship also led to some New York Rangers hockey coverage for WINS and me, though frankly, I hardly knew the game at all. I learned fast when WINS secured the rights for the 1962 Stanley Cup playoffs, in which the Rangers had secured a berth. With only a week's notice that I had to broadcast a game with the Detroit Red Wings, I dashed to the Garden for my first full look at a hockey game. A few days later I was on a train to Detroit poring over the NHL rulebook (along with the help of a grade-school primer on the sport). By the time I walked into the Detroit Olympia, I felt that I knew enough not to embarrass myself or insult my listeners. Then the darn Rangers went and got themselves into the Stanley Cup finals against the Montreal Canadiens. With a mere handful of games under my belt, I was shuttling between Madison Square Garden and the Montreal Forum broadcasting the Stanley Cup Championships! Talk about having to rise to the occasion!

So it was the Yankees in the spring, Giants and Yankees through the baseball season, the football Giants in the fall, and the Knicks and Rangers through the New York winters. On top of this schedule were my regular daily and weekly sports shows, plus the odd special project. There was also one more routine assignment in this busy schedule that was a labor of love—Monday Night Fights at the Eastern Parkway Arena in Brooklyn. I had to drive all the way over the Brooklyn Bridge, past Ebbets Field, to Pitkin Avenue (famous as the home of the "Murder Incorporated" syndicates) for an hour of air time, nine to ten o'clock. The boxing was tremendous. Eastern Parkway Arena was a major training and proving ground for future champions: Hurricane Jackson, heavyweight; Joey Maxim, light heavyweight; Archie Moore, who faced Teddy Yaroz for a heavyweight championship opportunity; and the future heavyweight king, Floyd Patterson, who would soon face Archie Moore for the heavyweight championship title vacated by the retiring Rocky Marciano.

The fans were almost as entertaining as the fights. They were wonderful East End characters right out of a 1930s B-movie. I even brought Lila to the arena one night, just to experience the atmosphere. She was thoroughly unimpressed and spent the entire evening at ringside reading a novel, certainly a first for the Eastern Parkway Arena. (Lila, who deplores violence of any kind, agreed to join me for just two more of the many fights I called over my career. Lila and I saw our old acquaintance from Honolulu, Carl "Bobo" Olson, face Archie Moore at the Polo Grounds. Moore devastated him. She joined me some years later for the Muhammad Ali–Brian London fight from London's Wembley Arena, a fortunate chance to see Ali at the very top of his form.)

But Brooklyn wasn't a jumping-off point just for great boxers; it proved to be the same for at least one boxing announcer. When Floyd Patterson made it to the world heavyweight championship, so would I.

It could all only have happened in New York City: young broadcaster comes to town, meets the greatest in the business, covers some of the game's best in every major sport, and is recognized in restaurants from Pitkin Avenue to Manhattan.

And baby, this kid felt like he was on top of the world!

The Next Best Thing to Being There

The art and politics of baseball re-creation

DURING MY FIRST few years in New York there were great machinations afoot in and around the city's two National League teams. The post–World War II boom brought new people and new businesses to the West Coast. Great opportunities for both budding and longtime sports franchises existed in the West. So after a half century in Brooklyn, owner Walter O'Malley announced that the Dodgers were moving to Los Angeles, and almost simultaneously Horace Stoneham revealed plans to move his Giants to San Francisco. Overnight, there was to be no National League representation in the country's greatest city, and New York was a National League town. People adored these teams. Now, decades of tradition and fandom were coming to an end. The shock and outrage of the teams' fans created an East Coast opportunity for WINS.

At WINS, we were in a pretty good position because we had the Yankees, and they would become the only game in town.

As previously stated however, WINS was owned by one J. Elroy McCaw, and "pretty good" wasn't what he had in mind for his dreamchild. What he had in mind was either madness or genius, or a little of both.

We had just moved the location of the station from West 44th Street down to Columbus Circle, 59th and Broadway. One day Elroy invited me out for a cup of coffee and as we sat down, asked me, "Les, who do you want to broadcast this summer, the Giants or the Dodgers?"

Now, Elroy wasn't a real dyed-in-the-wool sports fan—he was a broadcaster—but it seemed inconceivable to me that he hadn't heard about the pending departure of the two ball clubs. Nevertheless, not wanting to embarrass him, I began to explain about the plans of Walter O'Malley and Horace Stoneham. He cut me off instantly.

"I *know* where they're going!" he said, "What I *want* to know is which team you'd like to broadcast this summer."

My mind couldn't quite get into gear on this conversation. What was he asking? Was he thinking of sending me to the West Coast? I had just come from there! Unless . . .

"Wait a minute, Elroy, are you thinking what I think you're thinking? Because if you are it won't work. It just won't work!"

"It *will* work" he replied. "You're going to re-create the games here in New York. And it's going to make WINS and Les Keiter famous!"

Baseball re-creations are today little more than a footnote in radio broadcasting history. Studio re-creations were born in the 1920s when commercial radio was just beginning to take on the role of providing information to the mass public, a role that previously had belonged exclusively to newspapers and magazines. A few cities boasted radio stations that might broadcast live from a ballpark now and again (the first live radio baseball broadcast was alleged to be broadcast by KDKA in Pittsburgh), but even these pioneers couldn't do anything about "away" games—the technology simply didn't exist to pick up a decent signal from another city—and small cities couldn't get access to major league sports broadcasts at all. The public, however, had decided they liked to listen to sports on the radio and demanded more.

Cross-country communication was done by wire, telegraph, and the printed word. Somewhere along the line, announcers began to dramatize the details of a game and eventually the entire game, inning-by-inning, pitch-by-pitch, and re-creates came into being. In the 1930s, baseball re-creations were commonplace, and all the old-time sportscasters did them—Ernie Harwell, Russ Hodges, Mel Allen, Red Barber, and the other greats of their era.

It was at that time that I did *my* first re-creations—as a kid listening to the radio in my bedroom, emulating Seattle sports legend Leo Lassen as he broadcast the games of our local ball club. I clipped box scores from the paper and kept my own scorebooks of my favorite teams. As I mentioned earlier, I had a child's baseball game with dice that would roll out strikes and balls and hits, and as I played the game, I'd announce the entire affair, imagining it all in my head, copying the rhythm and phraseology of Leo Lassen as the game progressed.

Fifteen years later, my childhood re-creations would all come back when I broadcast my first season of Class-A baseball with the Modesto Bees. I broadcast the home games live and re-created the road games. Sitting in the studio, I received a wire-copy rundown of the game: who pitched? who batted? did they strike out, walk, or hit? who scored? Everything else was from my knowledge of the team, a couple of cheap sound effects (a drumstick, a woodblock and some crowd noise), and a fertile imagination.

When a re-create is done right, the audience forgets that it is not listening to live play-by-play. If a re-create is done wrong, it sounds like . . . well, it sounds like an idiot in a radio studio reading wire copy. The difference between the two is a matter of preparation, concentration, accuracy, a certain dramatic flair, and most of all, caring about what you're doing. I cared about it. A lot of broadcasters did re-creates back then; I'm proud to say I did them well.

The scariest thing about the process, of course, is the chance of losing track of the game: the count, the batting order, whether a batter hits right-handed or left-handed. I've seen re-creators use all manners of systems to stay on track. Some broadcasters would use little models of a baseball diamond and pieces with the players' names on them. They would move the players to their positions so they would remember who was where. Other broadcasters developed a system of colored lights to keep track of the action. For me, it was just a matter of keeping a good scorebook and jotting down the events as I read them off the wire copy. To make the game more interesting, I'd use programs and news clippings to provide color (". . . here comes Stevens off the bench, he's wearing what he calls his lucky number twenty-two," or "Reese is back in the lineup tonight after three days off with a sore shoulder . . ."), and maybe even a photo snapshot of the stadium to help visualize the event (". . . and it drops foul along the right field line, into the visitors' bullpen").

How close can you stay to the real game? It's hard to say. You *don't* know for instance, how many strikes and balls a batter might have on him before he hits the home run you *do* know he hit. But if you follow the team well, you might be aware that a particular player has a tendency to swing on the first pitch

Re-creating the Un-re-creatable

What happens when the wire services break down or the account of the game comes across the wires garbled? Les says you stall and hope the problem is corrected real fast!

Many times Les' listeners would hear that the manager goes to the mound, a coach goes to the mound, somebody goes to talk to the umpire, the batter fouls off several pitches, the batter breaks a bat, the catcher is hit with a foul tip, and so on. Anything to kill time until the technical problems are corrected.

The garbled account creates another sort of problem. Keiter had a surprising glitch come across the wires in a 1958 game during a Giants series with Cincinnati. Les recalled, "There were runners on second and third. Bob Schmidt was the runner on third. As things turned out, the pitch got away from Catcher Smoky Burgess and Schmidt scored on the passed ball. But the play came over the wire something like, 'Schmidt up, foul back into the screen. Singles back of plate. Error charged to Schmidt as Schmidt scored.' I stalled while yelling for the production engineer to have the wire service re-run the play."

Les Keiter interview, January 22, 1991

or hit a lot of fouls. You might *not* know what kind of pitch struck a man out, but you *remember* what a certain pitcher's key weapon is. You can't *see* the condition of a field after a rain delay, but you know from your *preparation* what condition the stadium usually is in when wet. You use all this research and experience to create a broadcast that may not be absolutely *correct* in every detail, but is certainly *plausible*.

I had done professional re-creates in Modesto, Hawaii, San Francisco, and occasionally in New York, doing American League games on the Yankees' travel days. But this new proposal from J. Elroy McCaw was simply overwhelming.

"Listen, Elroy," I told him as he sipped his coffee, "You've got to be out of your mind! This isn't Honolulu or Centralia-Chehalis, this is New York. And this isn't the 1930s or 1940s. Sports fans in Manhattan, New Jersey, and Westchester are just too sophisticated for re-creates!"

He pointed out that my occasional American League re-created games were accepted just fine. I shook my head. "That's a novelty, and it's not their home town players. You're talking about doing an entire season of a beloved team!"

"So which team should it be?" he repeated, unruffled.

I tried to be logical.

"Okay first of all, there's a time problem, Elroy. The night games on the West Coast don't even start until ten or eleven o'clock New York time. Even if I just wait for the first three innings to get in, we can't get on the air until one in the morning!"

"We won't wait. You're going to do it live."

"LIVE??!!"

"Right off the teletype. Batter by batter. At 11:15 every night."

"It can't work! New Yorkers simply won't buy it! I'll be a laughing stock! It will be a disaster for WINS!" I just couldn't believe this conversation was happening. I was going to be back in a small-town station before I knew it.

J. Elroy McCaw looked me straight in the eye. I'll never forget what he said. "It *will* work. It won't be a disaster. What it *will* do is make WINS radio a success and make Les Keiter the biggest name on the air in New York. You're going to be famous. Mark my words, your career is going to skyrocket. Now, I'm set up to make the deal with either team, three years, for a lot of money. I'm counting on my sports director to tell me what it's going to be. The Dodgers or the Giants?"

I was silent.

Then I replied, "The Dodgers are old. Jackie Robinson is old, Pee Wee Reese is old, Carl Furillo is old . . . the pitchers are old. The team is wearing out, and they've got to rebuild. The next few years will be losing seasons for them. And they are going to be playing at the Los Angeles Coliseum with that

Now Batting...

Here is your chance to re-create one half-inning in a St. Louis Cardinals–San Francisco Giants game I called in 1958. The game is being played in San Francisco. The copy is exactly, including misspellings and typographical errors, as it came over the Western Union wire.

FIRST STLOUIS

BLASINGAME UP BATS LEFT

B1 HIGH. HIGH FOUL BACK IN STANDS S1

S2 C. GROUNDED A FOUL PAST THIRD. B2 OUTSIDE

HIT BLASINGAME GROUNDED A SINGLE TO CENTER OVER SECOND BASE.

CIMOLI UP BATS RIGHT

HIT CIMOLI LINED A SINGLE TO LERT CENTER FIELDED BY BRANDT FIRST HOP AFTER LONG RUN . . . ON THE HIT AND RUN BLASINGAME WENT TO THHRD. THROW TO SPENCER AT SECOND.

MUSIAL UP BATS LEFT GETS A BIG HAND.

B1 LOWINSIDE. B2 LOW. GROUNDED A FOUL PAST FIRST. MILLER AND ZANNI WARMING FOR THE GIANTS.

HIT MUSIAL BLOOPED A SINGLE INTO SHORT LEFT NEAR THE LINE, SCORING BLASINGAME, CIMOLI NON SECOND.

BOYER UP BATS RIGHT.

B1 LOWINSIDE. S1 FANNED. B2 LOW. HIT BOYER DOUBLED TO RIGHT NEAR THE LINE BALL ROLLING NEAR THE CORNER SCORING CIMOLI AND MUSIAL HELD WAS UP AT THIRD.

big, high left-field fence just 290 feet from home plate, but the novelty of it will die quickly.

"The Giants? The players are young, so young that nobody has heard of most of them. But the youngsters they're bringing up have tons of potential. Players like Orlando Cepeda, Willie Kirkland, and Felipe Alou are going to be great. And they've

ALOU PEGGED TO SPENCER, RIGNEY WALKS TO THE MOUND.

THAT IS ALL FOR MCCORMICK . . . STU MILLER A RIGHT HANDER NOW PITCHING FOR THE GIANTS.

NO RECORD.

ESSEGIAN UP BATS RIGHT.

GROUNDED A FOUL BACK THE PLATE S1. S2 FANNED A HIGH SLOE CURVE. OUT S3 CALLED A CURVE ON THE OUTSIDE CORNER.

FLOOD UP BATS RIGHT.

B1 LOWINSIDE. CEEDXX CEPEDA AND SPENCER PLAYING IN

B2 LOWINSIDE. GROUNDED A FOUL A FOOT OUTSIDE THIRD BASE. S1. OUT FLOOD POPPED TO RODGERS BACKING UP IN SHORT LEFT.

H SMITH UP BATS RIGHT

S1 FANNED B1 LOWINSIDE. B2 LOW. SIDE RE-TIRED, H SMITH FLIED TO BRANDT IN MID LEFT.

TWO RUNS FOUR HIT NO ERRORS TWO LEFT

The wire copy comes to me a batter at a time. By the time I go on the air I might be two or three batters behind. So to avoid making a mistake by giving out action that has not yet taken place I have the copy placed face down in front of me. I read only the information on the batter at the plate and re-create the action related to his turn at bat. I do not want to know how things are going to come out in advance any more than the listener does. The above half inning took almost fifteen minutes to re-create. Try it!

From Les Keiter's scorebook

got the brightest star in baseball today, Willie Mays, who simply owns New York. Even if fans don't miss the team, they're going to miss Willie. If you are determined to do this, San Francisco is the team whose games we should re-create."

Within the week, WINS penned a deal with Giants executive Chub Feeney for the broadcast rights and another with Tom Villante at advertising giant BBDO for sponsorship. Me? I was still leery about the entire proposition.

"You're going to be the biggest name in New York," Elroy repeated on countless occasions. I wanted to believe him, and had reason to trust him—he was a genius in the world of radio and (later) television. He and Jack Keating had bought WINS from the Crosley Corporation for $400,000 in 1952. It was already worth twice the purchase price. In ten years Elroy would sell WINS to Westinghouse for nearly $11 million! J. Elroy McCaw knew his stuff. So I went along, laying my very career on the hope that he was right.

Opening day came for the Giants' 1958 season. They were playing at the Pacific Coast League Seals Stadium at 16th and

A Fan's Reaction

Sports Department: Baseball
WINS
New York, N.Y.
Dear Sirs:
Just a line of appreciation for your re-creations of the San Francisco Giants' baseball games. I know of a whole host of listeners in the greater Hartford area who have enjoyed listening as much as I have. And please pass the word to Les Keiter that we think he is the *greatest*. He puts a dramatic wallop into a game ("Back, back, back, BOOM off the wall") that most broadcasters don't give to live action! So we're 100% behind having you broadcast all the Giant games you possibly can in 1960 and for many years to come. Old Giant fans never die!

Letter received, October 12, 1959

Bryant streets in San Francisco; Candlestick Park wouldn't exist for several years yet. The teletype brought the game to me at 11:15 at night, and I Keiter-ized it for New York City and beyond. An unknown slugger named Orlando Cepeda, nicknamed the Baby Bull, captured the imagination of the San Francisco and New York fans. At season's end he was voted Rookie of the Year. Willie Mays did what Willie Mays always did, and he now owned the Bay Area along with New York. And Elroy was utterly and completely vindicated in his convictions. For three years, Les Keiter's voice echoed up and down Broadway from every tavern and every taxicab until one o'clock in the morning. I was the voice of the National League in New York City, and the WINS re-creates of the adored Giants received higher ratings than Mel Allen's live games with the (oft-despised) Yankees. To my genuine surprise I became the darling of both the sports columnists and the entertainment columnists. I suppose they didn't quite know which category my re-creations fell into. The whole idea was a masterstroke from a master broadcaster, Mr. J. Elroy McCaw.

Television and satellite technology would make re-creates an anachronism in the following decades, though as late as 1987 I would continue to do them, covering road games for the Triple-A Hawaii Islanders in Honolulu. As well as providing local listeners with a dose of evening baseball, these recent re-creates became a point of curiosity for news and feature reporters, and I found myself doing versions of them for NBC's Tom Snyder, Roy Firestone on ESPN's "Sportslook," Larry King on "Larry King Live," Jack Perkins on the "NBC Nightly News," and "The Today Show" with Tom Brokaw. Brokaw commented to Jane Pauley after my feature that "Neil Armstrong didn't really walk on the moon . . . Les Keiter re-created the whole thing!" I took that as a compliment.

Re-creations are still fun to do, and I love showing younger sportscasters a bit of their own history—how we "got by" without high technology and ESPN.

And looking back, I guess we "got by" just fine, thank you.

A Childhood Dream Fulfilled

*Yankee Stadium and the three Patterson vs. Johansson
fights (plus John Wayne, William Holden, and
Howard Cosell thrown in for good measure)*

BOXING IS WITHOUT a doubt the most basic of sports. Two in-
dividuals climb into a ring and fight until one no longer can.
That's about it . . . not too many rules, but lots of action. Is
the sport too brutal as many complain today? Perhaps. Mainly
it just *is* what it *is*, no polish and no apologies. Boxing.

I've followed the sport since I was a youngster. I was
drawn to it—strictly as a spectator—while growing up. Two of
my heroes were Freddy Steele and Al Hostak, popular Seattle
world boxing champions. I remember coming home from Camp
Orkila as a kid because my dad wanted me to see Freddy
Steele's fight with Hostak—the big meeting between rival
hometown favorites. Freddy Steele had won the middleweight
championship title from Ken Overlin some years before and
instantly became the number-one sports figure in Seattle. Steele
was a smooth, practiced veteran. He was clean-living, handsome,
and he became my first real hero. Young Al Hostak was the

tough kid on the block, from Seattle's Georgetown District, and a real knockout puncher. A rivalry had developed, and they were destined to meet, though most thought Hostak was too green to face Steele. The pre-fight hoopla was crazy. The promoters brought in the already-legendary Jack Dempsey to referee the fight—and that alone was enough to bring me down from my beloved summer camp.

The Steele-Hostak bout was the first fight I ever saw, and I'll never forget it. It was outdoors at Seattle's Civic Center. I was amazed to see a whole stadium full of people who were there just to watch two boxers face off man-to-man. The bell rang, and twenty seconds into the first round Hostak threw a vicious punch. Steele was knocked flat, and *no one* ever had seen Freddy Steele down. The crowd was stunned. Steele got up and got knocked down again. It seemed to my young eyes that Dempsey was always counting. Again and again Hostak put Steele on the canvas. There was no three-knockdown-and-out rule then. Finally Steele couldn't get up any more. It was the dethroning of a king, a new star on the rise, and the audience mirrored the mixed emotions of the occasion: cheers for Hostak, a come-from-nowhere Rocky story if there ever was one, and sadness for the old warrior, who would never be able to come back again.

As for me, tears were rolling down my cheeks after seeing my hero so thoroughly beaten. But there was something else I felt, too: the thrill of the occasion, the fans packed shoulder-to-shoulder, and the utter power of the sport. I thought "this is something I like, this is something I want to do, broadcasting fights, *that's my dream!*" The next summer I stated my goal to broadcast from Yankee Stadium. Of course, I thought it would be baseball, but in fact, it would turn out to be boxing: Floyd Patterson vs. Ingemar Johansson, my first nationally broadcast championship fight.

Boxing has threaded its way through my entire career. I broadcast bouts in the Pacific over the Armed Forces Radio Network during the war. In Hawaii in 1949 and 1950, I announced many great fights at the old Honolulu Stadium and Civic Auditorium, including the fight won by Carl "Bobo" Olson over Teddy Yaroz. I broadcast all those Monday nights at the Eastern Parkway Arena in Brooklyn throughout the 1950s with the likes of Joey Maxim, Hurricane Jackson, and Floyd Patterson. And in 1958, after Patterson finally made his way to the championship, I got the nod, too.

Howard Cosell and me at ringside for the first Patterson-Johansson fight. We called the fight for ABC Radio.

ABC had heard my Monday night fights on WINS and, needing a blow-by-blow announcer, called me to meet with ABC Radio president, Bob Pauley. He told me they were entering into a series of nationally broadcast boxing matches and were seeking the right man to do their blow-by-blow. ABC sports director Howard Cosell would do color and analysis—and the commercials between rounds. It would be his first national assignment as well. I had known Howard through the sports broadcasters' weekly luncheons, and that was about all. But I had heard his weekly New York radio sports show—he was certainly knowledgeable and thorough—and was pleased to be paired with him. Shortly after that initial meeting, Les Keiter and Howard Cosell became the ABC Radio Network fight broadcasting team. (Chris Schenkel was the television fight broadcaster, also for ABC.) Our first fight would be a relatively minor matchup—as minor as any world championship fight can be—between unbeaten heavyweight champ Floyd Patterson and the virtually unknown Swede, Ingemar Johansson.

Patterson had won the vacant title after Rocky Marciano's retirement. Patterson defeated Archie Moore to become the youngest heavyweight champion ever. (A few years later, Cassius Clay—Muhammad Ali—would become the youngest heavyweight champion, a record that stood for nearly three decades until twenty-year-old Mike Tyson came along.) Since winning the championship, Floyd was an unstoppable, smooth fighter with a trademark leaping left hook that helped KO four opponents. Ingemar Johansson was the European heavyweight champion. Johansson had knocked out Eddie Machen back home in Sweden to win the title shot against Patterson. But it was the *way* he had laid Machen out that had the press buzzing. Johansson had an awesome right-hand punch—straight as an arrow and hard as a rock—that he called the "Hammer of Thor." It traveled about a foot and a half and was so fast you could barely see it. "I never know when it's going to land," he would say, talking about his own fist in the third person. When it did land, it was devastating: the opponent's lights would go out and stay out. The film of Machen's knockout had shown graphically what happens to a boxer on the receiving end of the Hammer of Thor. Machen was hit, lifted off his feet, and immediately fell to the canvas, absolutely unconscious. Machen came back to America to tell everyone who would listen what an awesome puncher Johansson was. And it was the Hammer of Thor that put the hype into motion for the fight. The promoters ran the film of Machen's fall in the window of Gimbels Department Store, and by fight week it was the catch phrase on everyone's lips.

There was more pre-fight hoopla to come. The bout was also tied up in a promotional campaign related to an upcoming Hollywood film called *The Horse Soldiers*, a Civil War epic starring John Wayne and William Holden. Wayne and Holden were also involved financially in the film, and somehow United Artists, their advertising agency, and ABC agreed that the fight would be a good way to advertise the upcoming release of the film, and Mr. Wayne and Mr. Holden were to be involved in the broadcast. I was asked to attend a meeting at the United Artists offices on Seventh Avenue in Manhattan to work out details of the two stars' involvement. Such a meeting I had never experienced, before or since.

On arrival I was escorted to a huge conference room and seated at a long, polished table. Some ABC executives were there along with Howard Cosell and Chris Schenkel. There were several representatives from the advertising agency and the studio, and finally, larger than life, John Wayne and William Holden. The two arrived and took seats at opposite ends of the very long conference table. Wayne was wearing a fedora hat that he never took off, mainly to hide his balding pate. After everyone was seated, a young executive in a gray flannel suit stood up to begin the meeting. He had barely started when one of the actors—I think it was Holden—produced a bottle of Scotch whiskey, took a swig, and then slid the bottle the length of the table to Wayne. After taking a slug, Wayne gave the bottle a mighty shove, and it skittered along the tabletop past all of us to Holden. Holden would take another swig, and off the bottle would go to Wayne. It went on and on. We all watched it like a tennis match, not saying a word. The young executive, clearly out of his league experience-wise, gamely went on with his little speech. The plan was for Wayne and Holden to voice a pre-produced opening for the broadcast that blatantly promoted their movie. They would attend the fight and be available between rounds for interviews with me and Howard Cosell on radio and Chris Schenkel on television. (The bottle continued to slide back and forth.) Then he started on the details. Mr. Wayne and Mr. Holden would arrive at Yankee Stadium by limousine at 9:30 P.M.; an ABC staff member would escort them to ringside, one to our radio desk, the other to the television position on the other side of the ring; at the end of the first round, the ABC escort would bring Mr. Wayne around the ring to Mr. Schenkel and bring Mr. Holden around to Mr. Keiter and Mr. Cosell; at the end of Round Two, Mr. Holden will be escorted to Mr. Schenkel, and Mr. Wayne to . . . etc., through a whole litany of useless details. Meanwhile, the bottle slid back and forth, the two stars didn't say a thing, and Mr. Gray Flannel Suit kept talking and talking. Suddenly, there was a huge BANG! of the bottle on the table. Holden stood up with a surly look on his face.

"ENOUGH! WE'VE SAT HERE AND LISTENED TO THIS BULLSHIT LONG ENOUGH! NOW *I'LL* TELL *YOU* HOW IT'S GONNA BE!!"

We listened.

"IN THE FIRST PLACE, JUST TELL ME WHAT TIME THE BELL RINGS FOR ROUND ONE. I DON'T WANT TO HEAR ABOUT ALL THAT HORSE MANURE AND INTRO-DUCTIONS . . . WHEN DOES THE BELL RING?"

"Between 10:15 and 10:30," an ABC executive timidly offered.

"FINE, LET'S SAY 10:20. AND YOU EXPECT US TO BE THERE AT 9:30? IN A PIG'S ASS! WE WILL ARRIVE

AT YANKEE STADIUM AT 10:10. AND WHEN OUR LIM-
OUSINE PULLS UP AT THE ENTRANCE THERE WILL BE
FORTY—FOUR, ZERO—UNIFORMED POLICEMEN TO ES-
CORT US—TWENTY FOR MR. WAYNE AND TWENTY
FOR ME. WHEN WE GET OUT OF THE CAR, THEY WILL
FORM A CIRCLE AROUND EACH OF US, AND WE WILL
GO DIRECTLY TO MY SEAT, AND MR. WAYNE'S BODY-
GUARDS WILL TAKE HIM DIRECTLY TO HIS SEAT!"

The gray flannel suit looked as if he might speak. He never
got the chance.

"I DON'T THINK YOU HAVE ANY CONCEPT OF WHO
YOU'RE TALKING TO!" Holden continued. "I COULDN'T
STEP OUT THE DOOR OF THIS BUILDING ONTO SEV-
ENTH AVENUE. PEOPLE WOULD JAM AUTOGRAPH
BOOKS IN MY FACE; THEY'D TEAR AT MY CLOTHES!
PEOPLE KNOW ME IN EVERY CITY IN THE WORLD. I
GET MOBBED WHEREVER I GO. AND THIS IS NEW
YORK!

"NOW I'M ONLY SIX FEET TALL. *THAT'S JOHN
WAYNE!* HE'S SIX FOOT, SIX. THEY SEE HIM COMING
EIGHT BLOCKS AWAY! AND YOU WANT US TO GO
WALTZING AROUND THE RING BETWEEN ROUNDS?
LIKE HELL! ANYONE WHO WANTS AN INTERVIEW CAN
BRING HIS MICROPHONE TO ME AND TALK TO ME IN-
SIDE MY CIRCLE OF FIVE COPS! DO YOU UNDER-
STAND?" And BANG! the bottle pounded on the table again.
"MEETING ADJOURNED! NOW WHERE ARE OUR BODY-
GUARDS TO TAKE US BACK TO THE HOTEL?"

And off they went, leaving a hushed gathering in their
wake. The plans were amended to Mr. Holden's specifications,
and the stir they caused on arrival and departure in the stadium
would prove him right. I've never seen such a mob scene.
Without bodyguards they would have been mauled. It all happened just like Holden said it would.

More hoopla. Johansson was training in upper New York
state at Grossingers Resort in the Catskill Mountains, and he
brought his whole family with him. Mother Johansson did all
the cooking—he didn't like the kosher food served at
Grossingers—whipping up huge batches of meatballs and the like
for the Scandinavian contingent. Rolph Johansson—the light-
heavyweight champion in Sweden—was Ingemar's brother and
a sparring partner. Both brothers brought their fiancées. Ingemar's

father and, of course, his trainer, Edwin Alquist, were there. Johansson worked out at the ski lodge, abandoned for the summer, and visitors were allowed free reign of the grounds— Wayne, Holden, Jack Dempsey, Eddie Fisher, and other entertainers from Grossingers and the neighboring resorts were seen regularly, as well as the press corps. I was there, accompanied by sons Marty and Ricky, who wound up sitting next to Dempsey. (Marty to Ricky: "Who *is* this guy?" Ricky to Marty: "That's Jack Dempsey, the former heavyweight champion!" Marty takes an appraising look at Dempsey. Marty to Ricky: "Was he any good?") The whole place had a carnival atmosphere.

Fight night approached. Yankee Stadium was sold out, and the radio and television audience promised to be huge. The evening arrived. The fighters were ready, the fans were ready, Howard and I were ready . . . and then the bout was postponed one day due to rain. The delay just added to the frenzy and my nervousness. This was, after all, my big night in the spotlight, too. After this I might be headed back to Centralia-Chehalis!

It was also the night I would fulfill my childhood dream: tonight, June 26, 1959, Les Keiter, thirty years out of Camp Orkila, would broadcast live from Yankee Stadium. Amazing!

On to the fight itself. Despite the Hammer of Thor hype, Patterson was still odds-on favorite. He was a superb athlete, a true boxer. Floyd used the peek-a-boo style taught to him by Cus D'Amato (who thirty years later would teach Mike Tyson the same technique). He used a severe crouch, bent real low, and bobbed and weaved like a dancer. Floyd was not a big man. At his top weight of 190 pounds, he was never really more than a slightly overgrown light heavyweight. But he was experienced, he was smart, he was smooth, and he had that leaping left hook that packed a terrific wallop. Johansson outweighed Patterson by at least twenty-five pounds. Unlike Floyd, he was flat-footed, a plodder who waited for the chance to use his right—the Hammer of Thor.

The bell rang, and the fight was finally underway. The fighters were cautious the first two rounds. The rounds were a study in contrast between the two fighters. Johansson seemed to tower over Patterson due to the size difference and Floyd's exaggerated crouch. The Swede used a good left jab to keep Patterson at bay but was never given an early opportunity to use his powerful right hand. Maybe there was no Hammer of

Thor after all? In any event, after two rounds there was little to choose between the two.

But in the third it happened. Just as the round got underway, Johansson saw his opening. The Hammer of Thor caught Patterson clean on the jaw. It was so explosive and so sudden that I bolted right out of my seat, as did everyone else in Yankee Stadium. Patterson was *on his back* and struggling to get to his feet again. Ingemar, who had knocked out more than a few people, but never in such a crowd, went absolutely bananas, forgetting all the basic rules of the sport. As Floyd slumped, Johansson continued to hit him—on the top of the head, behind the ears, on his back. He was like a guy in an alley who has a man down and kicks him and pounds on him until he doesn't move any more. Patterson was badly hurt. He didn't know where he was. His eyes were crossed and glazed. Most fighters would have been totally unconscious at this point. Patterson was surviving only on instinct, fighting for his life. Ruby Goldstein, the famous referee, managed to push Johansson to his corner. Goldstein then got totally confused and didn't know if the count was six or eight or nine. Just crazy! But we knew the Hammer of Thor had landed—it was real, and it happened just feet above my microphone! Patterson somehow managed to get back on his feet, and Goldstein motioned the boxers to continue. The blows kept on raining, nearly all of them from Johansson, most of them wild, but many finding the champion. Patterson again slumped to his knees, this time with arms clutched around Johansson's legs. Johansson just kept on punching as Floyd tried to shimmy up to his feet again. Two knockdowns . . . three . . . four! Patterson was helpless; he didn't know where he was, and he was bleeding from the mouth and eyes. Goldstein was trying to give the champ every chance he could to get out of trouble before he stopped the fight.

"How long can Floyd survive this?" I screamed into the microphone above the roar of the Yankee Stadium crowd. Ingemar got wilder and wilder and then incredibly, after a half round of being pummeled, Floyd looked like he had started to clear the cobwebs, like he might dodge his way out of the woods and—WHAM! The Hammer of Thor flew and landed again, and Patterson was knocked halfway across the ring and onto the ropes, slumped, staring glassy-eyed out into the crowd. Goldstein managed this time to get Johansson quickly into a neutral corner and returned to begin his countdown. Floyd managed to stand

Floyd Patterson is the recipient of the Hammer of Thor, thrown by Ingemar Johansson. My face is behind the ABC microphone. Note John Wayne just below where Floyd is about to fall.

on wobbly legs at about the count of eight. Goldstein looked into his eyes, and I thought that certainly this would be the end of the carnage. But he gave the champ one last chance and signalled to Johansson to commence boxing. Johansson came running across the ring, threw a right straight between Floyd's eyes, and—BANG! Patterson was down on all fours again, the sixth knockdown in the round. I was so wrapped up in the pandemonium I had climbed halfway onto the apron. Patterson struggled to his feet yet one more time—*how, I'll never know*. Johansson hammered him, knocking him down for the seventh time. This time Goldstein said it was over. The entire stadium was in an uproar—the loudest sound I ever heard. The Swedes piled into the ring. Johansson was mobbed. The ABC production crew was screaming into the headset for Cosell to get into the ring to interview the new champion. Howard couldn't get anyone who spoke English and Swedish to help him get through to Ingemar. Finally he elbowed his way close enough to hold his microphone at arm's length and called to Johansson at long range "Did he ever hurt you?" There was no response from the new champion. With that, Howard turned and saw two men utterly alone in the far corner of the ring, Cus D'Amato and Floyd Patterson, his head hung down, Cus's arm around his shoulder. I learned long ago, that in a boxing match, everyone streams to the winner; they don't care about anyone else. Cosell tried to get closer to them, but was pinned in the crush of humanity around him. So he yelled "Floyd!" four or five times in a rising crescendo as he forced his way nearer. Finally he was close enough to yell "Floyd, what happened?" And in a quiet, modulated voice, his eyes cast downward, Patterson replied:

"I got hit, Howard."

That said it all. And then D'Amato made his famous prediction. "I will tell you right now, that for the first time in the history of boxing . . . " (the crew-cut, old-time manager was indeed quite a student of the sport, and always spoke in this sort of senatorial style) ". . . for the first time in the history of boxing, you will see a defeated heavyweight champion win his title back! We are going to fight Johansson again, and Patterson will regain his title, and remember I told you here tonight!"

And though those brave words would be put to the test a year later, that night the words being repeated around the world were "the Hammer of Thor."

Ingemar Johansson was an overnight sensation, an instant celebrity. He was on everyone's invitation list. His romance with his Swedish fiancée Birget was mentioned in all the columns. He went to Hollywood to be entertained by stars, and even performed bit parts in a couple of Alan Ladd movies.

Patterson went into seclusion. He was a sensitive man who took defeat very hard. This was his first defeat ever, and for weeks Patterson shunned the press and avoided the public. But the brilliant Cus D'Amato was determined to make good his prediction at Yankee Stadium. And before too long, he had Floyd back in training for a rematch.

The rematch date was set even before the first fight, though few had expected Patterson ever to need it. And the hype for the next fight began the night the first fight had ended. The bout was planned for another New York location—the Polo Grounds, half a mile from Yankee Stadium—a full year after the first matchup, on June 20, 1960.

This time, it wasn't an unknown against the champ. People knew both fighters, and battle lines were soon drawn. There were doubters who still said that the Hammer of Thor was a hoax, that Johansson had simply gotten to the champion with a lucky punch that led to the following seven knockdowns. Others—perhaps a majority—believed that Johansson was unstoppable and that the Hammer of Thor would destroy Floyd a second time. Ingemar, with all of his celebrity friends, certainly *looked* like a champion. Floyd was as quiet and well-mannered as ever. He was never a cocky publicity seeker. In interviews he would always say "I have the greatest respect for Ingemar . . ." (never "Johansson," always "Ingemar") ". . . Ingemar has that great right, so I'm working hard to counter it." Then, as now, he was always a real gentleman.

Once again, ABC had Howard Cosell and me teamed up for the fight, and the second meeting began much like the first. Both fighters came out sparring cautiously, the flat-footed Johansson stalking the crouched, peek-a-boo style of Patterson. The one-punch fighter and the superlative boxer. Again, there was little to choose between the two after the first two rounds. And then once again, with a mighty, single punch, the carnage began.

The third round began like the others, the relentless Johansson following the bobbing and weaving former champion around the ring. The two boxers were in a clinch, waiting for the referee to part them, and I saw something that seemed to telegraph what was to come. Sitting ringside was veteran actor and died-in-the-wool boxing fan James Cagney, a close friend of Patterson. During the clinch, Cagney gave Floyd a huge wink. and Patterson, who usually was completely oblivious to anything besides his opponent, *winked back* as if to say "Don't worry, Jimmy, this time I'm in control." And a moment later he was.

The punch came as explosively as the now legendary Hammer of Thor, but this time it was Patterson landing the blow. His leaping left hook had swooped down and caught the Swede clean on the jaw, and Johansson went down while the Polo Grounds crowd went as crazy as Yankee Stadium had the year before. He was up after a five count, still groggy, and Patterson hit him with that amazing left again. The punch came down like a Michael Jordan flying slam-dunk, right onto Johansson's chin. He fell like a tree, hitting the canvas with a force that shook the entire ring. And he didn't move. At all. For minutes he lay unconscious, completely inert . . . except his right foot, which started to twitch. I was afraid he was dying. He had landed with such force that I thought he might have broken his neck. They called for an ambulance and brought a stretcher into the ring. After about five minutes, Ingemar regained consciousness, got to his feet and slowly left the ring under his own power.

Floyd Patterson and Cus D'Amato were free to celebrate the first-ever comeback win for a defeated heavyweight champion, a wonderful moment for two deserving masters of their respective trades.

Of course there *had* to be a rubber match. It was set for the next year, March 13, 1961, in the Miami Beach convention center.

By the turn of the decade, I had become a regular member of the ABC Radio team for the heavyweight championship. This fight would be my third for ABC, and *all* of them were Patterson-Johansson matchups; it would be Ingemar's third fight in America, and *all* of them were against Patterson. It promised to be a humdinger. Both fighters trained with an intensity few had ever seen before.

Just hours before the bout, my longtime friend, agent, and advisor Irwin Rosee said, "Les, I want you to watch the first round very carefully." We were walking into the arena together. "Something's going to happen."

"What are you talking about?" Of course I'd watch the first round carefully; I watched all of the rounds carefully. Did he know something? Was there some kind of fix? Of course not, that couldn't be!

"Just watch the first round. Be alert," he repeated, and then he left. After scratching my head for a few minutes, I put it out of my mind and went about the rest of my preparations.

This time there wasn't an actor at ringside, but former heavyweight champion Max Schmeling was there as a guest of the American Boxing Association to see his first title fight since his own loss to Joe Louis in 1938. The fans were, needless to say, well-primed for this third meeting between two champions and former champions. It was a true rivalry, and the betting was close to even money.

The bell rang. The first minute looked like it was going to be another early-rounds stand-off of Plodding vs. Peek-a-Boo. Then BANG! The Hammer of Thor struck, and Patterson was hit and knocked down. He was stunned but not destroyed, and he was ready to resume after the eight count. The referee waved them together, and moments later it happened again. WHAM!

Johansson's awesome right caught Floyd on the side of the face, and this time the champ was hurt. He fell against Ingemar, pinning the Swede's arms as he struggled to clear his head and stay on his feet. He managed to do it and raised his gloves once more. Twenty seconds later another huge punch—BANG! And now JOHANSSON WAS DOWN! Floyd's trademark left had caught him clean and laid him low. He managed to get to his feet just before the bell.

Between rounds, Cosell was going berserk as only Howard can: "THIS IS AMAZING! THIS IS THE MOST INCREDIBLE FIRST ROUND IN THE HISTORY OF BOXING!" Who can blame him? Thousands of fans around us were going just as crazy. As for me, I could hear Irwin Rosee's words echoing in my memory. How had he known?

The two fighters took their break standing up, glaring at each other with fire and blood in their eyes. What would happen next? In fact, the following four rounds showed none of the fireworks of the first. Johansson controlled much of the fight with his continuous pursuit and his jabs. Floyd was cagey behind his gloves. Going into Round Six, Ingemar's aggressiveness edged him ahead of the champion on points. I told the radio audience I doubted this fight would end in a decision. It didn't.

In the sixth round, Johansson threw a strong right punch that missed in a big way, bringing his shoulder and head down and past Patterson for a moment. It was all Floyd needed. He threw a rabbit punch that caught Ingemar just behind the ear, and the contender was instantly knocked to his hands and knees. On the six count he started to get up, shakily. By eight he began to get his feet under him. As the referee brought his hand down for the ten, he stood up. But he was too late, the referee called him out, and the fight went to Patterson. Argument and confusion ensued, but the call had been made. Floyd Patterson had retained the heavyweight championship title.

After the fight, I asked Max Schmeling about the call, and in his thick German accent he said, "Yah, I know that punch. It leaves your head clear, but your legs and arms won't move for you! It's terrible!" Was Johansson up too late for the count? "Yah," said Schmeling. Later that evening, I asked Irwin Rosee how he had predicted the first round.

"I visited their camps," he said, "and I'd never seen such ferocity." Usually by the last week, the training backs off to shadow boxing and light sparring, but Ingemar and Floyd were still at full throttle up to the day of the fight. "They were just too wound up," Rosee continued. "Something had to happen, and it had to happen fast!" He was right.

Ingemar Johansson continued his minor movie career and fought a few more fights in this country before returning to his homeland. He never got another chance at the title. Patterson would soon face the fearsome Sonny Liston, who had been in prison during the Johansson series.

As for me, I was facing more big fights and a host of changes, including the biggest disappointment of my career and a move away from New York.

Opportunity Knocks

The AFL, the Mets, and another move

IT WAS MY BASEBALL re-creations that reputedly attracted the attention of a man who played one of the most confounding roles in my career—Harry Wismer. Wismer was one of the old-time great announcers while I was growing up. He was one of the three big network radio voices for college football: Ted Husing on CBS, Bill Stern on NBC, and Harry Wismer on ABC. When I arrived in New York, their on-air careers were winding to an end. The new lineup of sportscasters included Red Barber, Mel Allen, Curt Gowdy, and others. It was at this point in broadcasting—the late 1950s to early 1960s—that many announcers were also making the transition from radio to the increasingly important medium of television. Names like Husing, Stern, and Wismer were still golden in the late fifties, and the fact that one of them was interested in me and my career was not to be shrugged off.

Burt Schulz, a colleague of mine at WINS who later moved

into the advertising field, was one of those people who seemed
to know everyone in and out of the broadcasting business. Burt
called one afternoon at the station and said, "Les, you're not
going to believe this, but I was just talking with Harry Wismer,
and he wants to meet you. He's become a real Keiter fan. He
wants to talk with you about something I think you should listen
to." Burt was vague on further details but set up a meeting for
me later that week at Wismer's Park Avenue apartment, just
steps away from the Waldorf-Astoria Hotel. As I walked into
the apartment building's lavish lobby I thought to myself that
Harry had done quite well for himself over the years.

When I arrived for the meeting, I was greeted by a secretary, a spectacular view of New York, and a booming voice I
recognized in a second. Harry Wismer hardly needed a microphone (and frankly, the same has been said about me); his voice
was huge, and for someone like me who had listened to him
for years, even decades, a recognizable trademark. The two of
us began to talk. Actually, Harry talked while I listened.

"I've been listening to your baseball re-creations, your
Knicks broadcasts, and the football with the Giants. I've listened
to your boxing matches. I'll be blunt. I think you're the next
big star in the sports broadcasting business!" I was no longer
the new kid in town, but this was, nevertheless, pretty heady
stuff to hear from a boyhood idol.

"I think that you're going to be the next Harry Wismer!"
This was a little harder to sort out. First of all, Harry's best
days had passed; mine were still building. I wasn't sure the
listening world wanted "the next Harry Wismer," or that I wanted
to be the same. Second, there was a touch of Harry's ego in
the statement that I should have recognized as a warning.

"Les Keiter is the next Harry Wismer, and it was Wismer
who discovered you." This was definitely an overstatement. I
was heard by millions of people every week, so I was somewhat
beyond discovery. But the view was great, the setting was re-
laxing, and I was curious about where this talk was leading. I
soon found out.

"I'm about to launch a brand new football league, one that's
going to make the NFL look sick."

Oh Lord, not that again. You see, the idea of a rival
football league for the NFL wasn't a new phenomenon.
Throughout the 1950s, just as today, it seemed a football season
never began or ended without someone talking about a new

league with new cities, new franchises, and a higher level of play. I had reported on the various plans and rumors on my WINS broadcasts for a number of years, and every attempt turned out to be a house of cards—the first breeze of reality would topple the entire scheme, at least until the next season. I wasn't interested in being one of those cards, especially since I was happily employed in the NFL with the Giants. But I listened. With Harry's voice you didn't have much choice, anyway.

He went on to paint a beautiful picture of the new league he envisioned and the people he was working with: Bud Adams in Houston, Ralph Wilson in Buffalo, Barron Hilton in Los Angeles, Billy Sullivan in Boston and Lamar Hunt in Dallas. All were important and influential businessmen with the financial resources needed to bankroll a football team. Many, in fact, had been hoping to purchase established NFL franchises but had been unsuccessful. "These are the people," Wismer said, "who are going to storm the front of the National Football League and beat the owners at their own game! And Les Keiter is the man who is going to sell this league to New York and the rest of the nation! You're our broadcaster! You're my man!"

I tried to explain that it was impossible for me to even consider it. I had a contract with the New York Giants and their owners, the Mara brothers, but he countered with more of his plans for the new league.

"Les, we're going to scout out the best new young players in the country, people the NFL has never even heard of! And we're going to bring back some of the greats who still have it, like George Blanda, Tobin Rote, and Jack Kemp. It's going to happen, and I need you to sell it to New York." There was that "sell it" phrase again. I told him the time-honored "I'll think about it and get back to you" line, knowing that I wouldn't. We shook hands, and I left and headed back to the station, doubting I would hear much of it again. I was wrong.

Harry called weekly to keep me informed of the league's progress, and over time the pretty picture he described actually began to take form. A commissioner was named: Joe Foss, the war hero. Teams were formed: the Los Angeles Chargers, the Dallas Texans, the New York Titans, the Oakland Raiders, the Boston Patriots, and others. A businessman named Al Davis started up the Oakland team on the West Coast. Wismer himself was one of the owners of the New York team. Great coaches like Sammy Baugh, Sid Gilman, and Hank Stram were hired.

Some recently retired NFL players like George Blanda were enticed back. So to most people's surprise, a real live rival football league inched its way to reality. It was the birth of the AFL—the American Football League.

Wismer never let up. He wanted me as the radio and television voice of the New York Titans. He asked me to go to a league meeting at the New Yorker Hotel. ABC executives Roone Arledge and Chet Simmons were there. ABC was putting together a national television broadcast package for the league. Over lunch, Simmons, who I barely knew, came up to me and said, "Harry Wismer is pushing you to become the national voice of the league." This was the first I had heard about this; Wismer had talked to me about broadcasting just the New York Titans' games. "He's pushing hard," Simmons continued, "and I'm telling you right here and now, it's not going to happen! We're hiring Jim Simpson for the league announcer. Harry Wismer is not going to dictate to us!"

I told Chet that it was fine with me. I still had no intention of leaving my job with the NFL and the Giants, anyway. We parted in a friendly enough fashion, and I left more convinced than ever that I'd never work with the new AFL. I was also beginning to realize that Harry Wismer's enthusiasm for me was beginning to ruffle some folks the wrong way. So it was with a great deal of surprise that I received a phone call the next week from ABC.

"I'm calling from Mr. Simmons' office," a woman informed me. "Mr. Simmons would like you to be the voice of the American Football League for ABC Television. You will be doing play-by-play for the season . . . " and she went on to describe the terms of the job, the salary, the whole works. I was more than a little confused. As I recalled, Chet had been adamant that I would *not* be the voice of the AFL. The woman on the phone knew nothing about my conversation with Chet Simmons. "Mr. Simmons would like to know if you're interested," she concluded. Of course I was, but there were some things to straighten out first.

I had talked to the Giants owner Jack Mara about the Titans' offer some weeks before to let him know that I wasn't interested in broadcasting the New York AFL franchise. I was the Giants' man. Now I went to see Jack again to talk about this new turn of events. The offer would be hard to pass up: national network television, an enormous amount of money

1960 HOME SCHEDULE

TITANS OF NEW YORK

at the POLO GROUNDS

SEPT. 11 — BUFFALO	SUN.	
16 — BOSTON	FRI. NITE	
23 — DENVER	FRI. NITE	
OCT. 23 — HOUSTON	SUN.	
28 — OAKLAND	FRI. NITE	
NOV. 4 — LOS ANGELES	FRI. NITE	
NOV. 24 — DALLAS		
THANKSGIVING DAY		

The birth of the AFL New York Titans. (L–R) Me, Titans co-owner Dr. Fred Crescente, AFL Commissioner Joe Foss, and Titans co-owner Harry Wismer.

(compared to my radio salary), and being in on the ground floor of what was promising to be an exciting league. Jack was terrific. He shook my hand and said "Les, you've got to do it. As much as I want you for my New York radio broadcasts, you just can't compare that to national television, a game every Sunday. You just can't say 'no,' " and with a handshake my contract with the Giants was dissolved. General Manager Ray Walsh joined us and added, "Les, just promise us one thing. Keep us informed about what's going on. Keep us posted. We hear a lot of rumors about some dirty tricks going on with the recruitment of coaches, officials, players, and college players. Let us know if you hear of anything."

I said I would, and fortunately it was a promise that was easy to keep. The new owners kept the image of the league clean, and all their recruiting was in compliance with league rules. The AFL had done what no rival league had done before. They had attained legitimacy. And much to my surprise, I was the official television network announcer for the new league.

Monday through Friday I continued my sports director's duties at WINS radio. Saturday and Sunday were devoted to the American Football League and the ABC Television Network broadcasts.

Wismer, naturally, invited me over for a champagne celebration. He was glowing in his triumph. I'll never know what he did to put me in the announcer's seat with ABC, but he was full of himself and ready to steer his new "protégé's" career onward and upward. "Les, you're my boy! You are the new Harry Wismer!" I was beginning to get worried about that line.

I went to work preparing for the AFL's inaugural football season. Chet Simmons would be the producer for the games, and whatever unpleasantness had led to my selection over Jim Simpson was never mentioned. Simmons was a real professional and would prove it over and over again in his career. We were broadcasting a sixteen-week season, a game every Sunday, from virtually every city in the league: Los Angeles, Buffalo, Dallas, New York, Oakland, Denver, Boston, Houston, and so on. Our first game was in Denver, the Broncos against the Boston Patriots. The anticipation for the AFL season was high, and the game did not disappoint. This was my first time announcing play-by-play for television, and I pretty much went about it as I would have done for radio. This was still a few years away from instant replays. It went well enough. After the game, Simmons and I watched the tape, and he suggested that I should tone things down a bit. This was television. I didn't have to be the eyes and ears for the fans anymore—they could see for themselves. The television audience needed a little less detail and a little more background. I agreed that his comments made sense. I toned down my play-by-play announcing for the next week's game.

Chet was happy with the results. A chemistry with my color commentators was developing—former quarterback George Ratterman and fullback Bill Dudley would be my most frequent partners that year—and we began to settle in for the season. But as soon as I got back to my hotel, Harry Wismer called. "What the hell was that?" he bellowed, "*Who* the hell was that? I hired Les Keiter for his excitement and enthusiasm. You sounded like some journeyman announcer on the television. I hired you to sell the American Football League to the country, and that's what I need you to do!" Of course, he didn't want to hear anything about the difference between radio and television.

He just wanted that old-time excitement. So, in order to please Harry, I tried to do what I could to liven things up for the next broadcast.

This time, it was Simmons who was all over me. What had happened to the ideas we'd been talking about? I was back to my radio style again. So I backed off. And the next week Wismer was back on the phone. He wanted me to "sell the league." ABC just wanted me to "do the game." It was time to put a stop to all this.

"Harry, I appreciate everything you've done for me, I really do. But you didn't hire me. It says American Broadcasting Company on my paychecks. ABC wants me to do the game a certain way, and I happen to think they're right." He started in on the "next Harry Wismer" stuff again, and push came to shove. "No, Harry! I'm not the new Wismer, or the next Wismer, or any Wismer at all. The name's Les Keiter, and I've got a job to do. So please, STOP CALLING AND LEAVE ME ALONE!"

The calls didn't stop, but they slowed down. I sensed I had made an enemy, though I hadn't meant to. But I knew I was right. I had a job to do.

It was a great job.

Every Sunday it was a new city and a new stadium. Announcing from Mile High Stadium in Denver, the Cotton Bowl in Dallas, the Orange Bowl in Miami, and the Los Angeles Coliseum was fabulous. Fans began to recognize me in the stands and wave. (Thanks to television, living rooms from Boston to the Bay Area were graced with my visage.) The sports division at ABC was great to work with. My announcing on the national telecasts led to commercials for White Owl cigars on Henry Fonda's "The Deputy" every week; White Owl was one of the leading sponsors of the AFL. It was pretty heady stuff.

The level of play was very high for a new league. The NFL had in fact been ready for a rival. There was an abundance of athletic and coaching talent available, and a real desire for more teams in more parts of the country, much more so than when the World Football League limped into existence twenty-five years later. The AFL was a success story in the making, and it was exciting to be the person bringing the action to fans across the country every weekend.

The AFL broadcasts allowed me to bring another "first" into the national limelight. In mid-season ABC visited Houston, where the game would be held at Jeppesen Field, a high-school

field. Early Sunday morning I received a phone call in my hotel room. A man said he was in the lobby and would like to
speak to me before I left for the game. Could I spare a few
minutes? I thought it was a salesman of some kind (in fact, I
would be right on that count) and tried to brush him off. He
was insistent. "My name is Judge Roy Hofheinz, and I've got
something that is going to shake the American Football League,
and all of major league sports."

Well how could I turn *that* down? I invited him up.

I was already getting dressed for the game when he knocked
on the door. He re-introduced himself and I thought I recognized
the name. It turned out he was a former mayor of Houston. He
carried a sample case like a salesman, which he proceeded to
open as he talked. "We're going to revolutionize the sports world
with this concept, and it's going to happen RIGHT HERE IN
HOUSTON!" Did I mention that Roy Hofheinz was a Texan?

My curiosity was piqued, and I sat down at the coffee table
to see what the heck he was assembling from the sample case.
"The whole sports scene is changing," he explained, "It's going
to be a bigger business than ever in the next twenty years. More
sports, more fans, you name it. This AFL is just the beginning."
He was putting together a model of a sports stadium as he talked.
"And this is the place where people are going to be watching
all of these sports," he said as he put the last piece in place.

The last piece was a roof—a dome—that he gingerly placed
on top of the entire stadium. "No more worries about weather.
We can play in the summer rain or the winter snow, day or
night, under perfect climate-controlled conditions. This is the
future of sports. And we're going to build the first one right
here in the city of Houston!" He went on to describe the con-
sortium he was heading up to get the domed stadium financed
and constructed. The longer he talked, the clearer it became that
Judge Roy Hofheinz wasn't just some nut off the street. I called
up Chet Simmons, and asked him to come to my room.

"We have to leave in a half-hour, Les," he complained,
but I convinced him it was important. He showed up five minutes
later, and Hofheinz gave him the short version.

"I'd like to show this during the game today," I told
Simmons and Hofheinz. "How about an interview with the judge
to show off this model. Can we do it?" It took some scrambling
over the next few hours, but it was finally arranged for the halftime break. I met Judge Roy Hofheinz at the fifty-yard line and

we talked for about five minutes on national television about his new dream. That was the first look America had at what would become the Houston Astrodome. The country-wide exposure was just what the former mayor had needed to generate enough excitement to bring his project into being. It would be nearly a decade before the dome was actually constructed and opened, and along the way Judge Hofheinz endured serious financial and health problems. But in the end, he would be proven right. Domed stadiums were the future. The Astrodome would be followed in time by Superdomes, Metrodomes, Kingdomes, and You-Name-It-Domes, until the opening of the Skydome in Toronto, which reverses the trend somewhat. (The Skydome opens up to the daylight or is closed, depending on the weather and insect conditions in Toronto.) But Houston's dome was first, and it is still a wonder to behold. Hofheinz called the Astrodome "The Eighth Wonder of the World," and one can forgive him the exaggeration. I would broadcast the first major sports event in the Astrodome in 1966—Muhammad Ali against Cleveland "Big Cat" Williams (and a fight several years later between Ali and Ernie Terrell)—and it was thrilling to be inside the structure that I first beheld as a table-top model.

The rest of the season passed. Chet Simmons and ABC were supportive to the end, but it was clear they still wanted their own man in the booth for the next season, and with Harry Wismer no longer my "champion," I knew my time as the AFL's national broadcaster was over. I had been at the center of too many hassles, none of them my own making. So at the end of the first season I was out. But it had been worth it. The new league had proven its viability. I had proven I could competently handle play-by-play on national television. And my job at WINS was still a daily challenge. I had no regrets. The AFL would eventually merge with the NFL, sparked by a disagreement from Oakland Raiders owner Al Davis, who "stole" quarterback John Brodie from the San Francisco 49ers. The ensuing arguments and lawsuits were settled with the merger. New commissioner Pete Rozelle established himself as the power in the combined NFL, and Al Davis remains to this day professional football's most ardent critic and maverick.

Roone Arledge emerged from the AFL dealings as the top dog of sports broadcasting. Chet Simmons was soon to be the sports director of NBC, and years later, ESPN. The New York Titans became the New York Jets, and with players like wide receiver Don Maynard, and later "Broadway" Joe Namath, they soon rivaled the Giants for home-town popularity.

Harry Wismer continued to call me up with advice or to request a favor. The phone calls came when I least expected them and continued for years. Harry just wasn't going to let me out of his life. To this day, I have very mixed feelings about the man. He led me to a wonderful opportunity and then made it impossible for me once I arrived. I gave up my job with the Giants for the AFL, and then the AFL was gone via the merger. I had tasted excitement and disappointment in equal doses, and for the time being, I was ready to concentrate on my job at WINS. But more excitement—and later disappointment—was to arrive before the AFL season finished.

The job I had always wanted most in sports was to do play-by-play of a major league baseball club, but it had always eluded me. Just before the Brooklyn Dodgers pulled up stakes in New York, they began looking for a broadcaster to team with Red Barber. The Dodgers owner Walter O'Malley called up Tom Villante at ad giant BBDO and said, "Get me Keiter!" But Tom (as he told me to my astonishment a decade later) told O'Malley I wasn't ready yet. "Let him season a few more years, Walter, then bring him up." They turned instead to Al Helfer, who finished the season for them. I was no longer in the picture the next year. The Dodgers hired a guy named Vin Scully. Vin was immediately accepted by the Dodgers' fans and moved with the team to Los Angeles in 1958. I never knew I was considered for the Dodgers' broadcasting spot before the man who in time would become *the* play-by-play man of baseball. Scully is one of the best ever, and it's impossible to imagine the Dodgers without him, but I like to dream what the team of Keiter and Scully (okay, Scully and Keiter) might have accomplished in sports broadcasting!

But in 1962 my number came up again. The major leagues were expanding, with plans to establish new franchises in several cities. Coincidentally, Houston was one of the expansion cities, and the team there would eventually take on the name of the stadium they played in: the "Astros," for the Astrodome. (They actually started off as the "Colt 45s.") The other new clubs would be the Minnesota Twins, the Texas Rangers, and New York, which would finally get a National League team to replace their beloved Dodgers and Giants. This new team would be called the Mets.

Expansion baseball teams are sometimes as shaky as start-up leagues, but from the very start the Mets looked like a class act. Joan Payson was the principal owner of the Mets. Bill Shea was building a stadium for the new team to play in. Casey Stengel, who had lost his job with the Yankees but was still loved by New Yorkers, was brought in as field manager. Rheingold Beer was signed as the main sponsor (a major beer sponsor was almost as important as a stadium for a new ball club), backed by their advertising agency, BBDO, and my old acquaintance, Tom Villante.

Things had changed since I lost the Dodgers job opportunity to Al Helfer and Vin Scully. I had been the city's voice for National League play with my Giants re-creations. I had paid my dues. I had obtained the "seasoning" that Villante thought I needed three years before. It was the zenith of my career when I was approached to be the play-by-play announcer for the New York Mets.

My partner in the booth was to be Ralph Branca, the former Dodgers pitcher. Branca was best known throughout baseball as the pitcher who had the bad luck to throw the pitch to Giants slugger Bobby Thomson that became the "home run heard round the world" and knocked the Dodgers out of the National League playoff in 1951. Since his retirement he had become an articulate, insightful baseball analyst with whom I was pleased to be teamed.

Lila and I were ecstatic. This was the job I had always wanted. For us, there was never a warmer winter in New York as we anticipated our first season in the majors and awaited the official announcement. It wasn't long in coming. Dick Young—without a doubt the best baseball writer of his time—"leaked" the story in the *New York Daily News*, and the congratulatory messages began to come in. Tom Villante called and told me to stay near a phone because they might want me at a press conference over the weekend. We settled in and waited for the call.

The call never came. I flew out to Los Angeles to do one of my last AFL broadcasts. An old friend, Lindsey Nelson, was in the next booth handling radio play-by-play. Prior to the broadcast, Lindsey and I were chatting, and I gave him some of the background information on my new job with the Mets. Lindsey suddenly took a deep breath and speaking just above a whisper said, "Les, I guess you haven't heard. The Mets officially announced their plans about an hour ago. They've offered me a three-year deal to do the play-by-play. I thought the job was yours, everybody did. And I want you to know I didn't have anything to do with it. I'm sorry."

I was devastated. I could hardly do the football game. My mind was completely on losing the one job I had always wanted. To this day I cannot remember broadcasting the football game. Of course, I knew Lindsey had nothing to do with the change in broadcasters. On reflection it had been a gutsy thing for him to tell me himself. But my disappointment overwhelmed me. I flew back to New York that night to tell Lila. She was in shock after hearing the news. I have never seen her so upset as she was that night and for months after. To this day Lila cringes when I recall the job that was not to be.

What happened? Apparently, sometime over that weekend, Rheingold Beer was dropped as the principal team sponsor, and BBDO, Tom Villante, Ralph Branca and I were sacked as well. On Monday morning, the J. Walter Thompson advertising agency announced that they would be bringing New York their first season of the New York Mets. Their broadcasting team would be Lindsey Nelson, Ralph Kiner, and Bob Murphy. As for the rest of us, it was back to the broadcasting showers. (Time would prove the Nelson-Kiner-Murphy partnership to be one of the most durable announcing teams in baseball. Lindsey Nelson stayed with the Mets until his retirement a few years ago, and Kiner and Murphy are still associated with the team.)

It was the lowest point of my entire career. If I had gotten the nod, who knows what direction our life might have taken? On the other hand, who knows what we might have missed? I've never been one for looking back and wondering "what if?" But I'll admit that this is the one situation I tend to wonder a lot about. Then, on the heels of this personal disaster came word that WINS was going to be sold to the Westinghouse Corporation, and the format changed to eliminate all of the sports broadcasts. So I not only lost the one job I always wanted; I was about to lose the sports directorship at WINS. But once again, just when my career seemed about to plunge, I got a call from the right person at the right time.

Philadelphia television executive Tom Jones called and asked me to lunch. We sat in a little Italian restaurant, and he came straight to the point. "We'd like you to consider becoming the sports director of WFIL, both the radio and television stations. We'd like you to move to Philadelphia." A week before,

The family is growing up. (L–R) Jodi, Ricky, Les, Lila, Barbara, Marty, and Cindy.

I would have laughed out loud at the idea of leaving New York. Now, I was interested in hearing more. The job would include evening television newscasts at six and eleven. I'd be doing fights, college basketball, college football, golf, the works. Philadelphia had just lost its NBA franchise when the Warriors moved to San Francisco, but it looked like another team was in the making. "You'd be doing it all. We're the number-one station in Philadelphia. We expect you to be the town's top sports announcer. Will you think about it?" I thanked him and told him I would.

"PHILADELPHIA!?" was the common reply in the family. The kids had all made good friends in our decade in New York. The younger twins were starting grade school, the older ones were almost in junior high school, Ricky was in junior high, and of course no one wanted to leave. Frankly, neither did I. But after another in a long tradition of "Keiter career summit talks," Lila and I decided it was opportunity knocking, once more.

It was time to close one chapter and open another. It was time to move on.

The Philadelphia Story

*Rodeos, road races, and the
glory days of the Big Five*

WE HAD BARELY SETTLED into our new home in the City of Brotherly Love when I was on the road again. My primary responsibilities were serving as the sports director of WFIL-TV and Radio, along with the full-time task of anchoring the sports desk for two daily television broadcasts. There was also the "side" business of Triangle Productions requiring my attention.

Triangle was a name applied to several arms of the Walter Annenberg empire, which also included *The Philadelphia Inquirer* and *Philadelphia Daily News* newspapers, and the WFIL stations. The most enduring Triangle company was Triangle Publishing and its *TV Guide*, the most widely read magazine in the country. Triangle Productions was a television company that produced syndicated programs for both regional and national distribution. A good number of the programs were sports specials.

Involvement in the Triangle Productions sports programs was part of my job—as if I weren't busy enough already! It was a typical Annenberg-ish thing to do. The attitude was "If they work for me, I'll tell 'em what to do!" We did, and he did. Thus began some of the strangest experiences I've ever had in sports broadcasting.

It began with auto racing. Now, auto racing is a wonderful sport for those who enjoy the speed and the noise and the endless tinkering with moving parts. I personally had never taken much of an interest beyond the names and results of the really big races, principally the Indianapolis 500 Auto Race. This mattered not to the folks at Triangle, and I found myself making the rounds of the American road racing circuit—Watkins Glen, Riverside, Elkhart Lake, the twelve hours of Sebring (imagine a sporting event twelve-hours long!). I had a commentating team that kept me up on the latest facts and figures, and I did solid work with my broadcasts—after all, a race is a race, whether on foot or on wheels, and an interview is an interview. And, like any sport, there's always some human drama to be discovered and described. That's where the truly interesting part of the game is to be found, even if I did split my eardrums trying to find it. I may not go down in racing history as Chris Economaki's or Jim McKay's equals, but I'm not embarrassed for my work in the field. Still, give me a ballgame any day.

There were friends to be found on the circuit too, and one of them has remained a very good friend through the years— Roger Penske. He was still a driver back then, one of the hottest in racing, and of course he would go on to be *the* impresario of American automobile racing: designing and building cars, managing teams and drivers, and promoting the entire sport. He also owned the largest Chevrolet dealership in Philadelphia, and was one of the movers and shakers in the city's business community. A remarkable man.

But if it's hard to imagine me in the noise, smoke and grease of pit row, try to picture me in cowboy boots and a Stetson hat! That was precisely my outfit when Triangle sent me to cover, of all things, the rodeo circuit. Yup, partner, it was the whole kit and caboodle: bronco busting, calf roping, steer wrestling, and riding Brahma bulls. (If you think that climbing in a ring with a Muhammad Ali or Mike Tyson is crazy, you should see one of those bulls at close range!) I think we did about thirteen rodeo programs at Jersey's Cowtown Rodeo, and they have come back to haunt me for decades, showing up as time-fillers on slow Sunday afternoons, or on

*Rope them little dogies! Ride 'em, cowboy! Wearing the
Stetson hat turned me into a true rodeo fan, and the words
just flowed.*

tiny UHF or cable television stations. I still run into folks who
recognize me as the guy with the white cowboy hat and microphone. I only wish I had residuals from all those broadcasts!

Sports specials were fun to do, but I preferred covering
the daily sports news and the local play-by-play. I was on WFIL
every evening, providing the sports news at six and eleven. I
also covered a lot of teams. I did the play-by-play of the fledg-
ling NBA 76ers basketball team. I also moonlighted by doing
play-by-play for TVS Sports, an independent television network,
and I broadcast regional and national college basketball for TVS'
"Game-of-the-Week." The man who owned TVS was Eddie
Einhorn, later a network television executive, and today co-owner
of the Chicago White Sox. He was also my employee for one
evening.

WFIL had sent me to New York for a live television
broadcast of the unbeaten basketball powers of the Ivy League:
Pennsylvania and Columbia. The ancient Columbia Gym would

be packed—it was a complete sellout—so Eddie Einhorn, a Penn Alumnus, called me up a few days before the game and said, "Les, you've just got to get me into that gym! I *have* to see that game!" I wanted to help but was unable to get Eddie a ticket. I told him I was sorry, but the place was absolutely sold out,

The Interview is Over

Whitney Reed is a 32-year-old professional tennis player known for his unorthodox shots and post-game partying. Following his semifinal victory in the 1961 Canadian Open, Reed attended a round of parties that continued until it was time to play the final. Despite the lack of sleep, Reed beat Mike Sangster of Great Britain. Unfortunately, his new training regimen knocked him out in the early rounds in 32 of 34 subsequent tournaments.

One win, however, was the Philadelphia Indoor Tennis Championship of 1963. After his semifinal win at the St. Joseph's Fieldhouse, Reed found himself back at the hotel snowbound and had no choice but to get some sleep. In the final he beat Frank Froehling to win a tournament he wasn't supposed to win.

After wrapping up the title he found himself being interviewed by Les Keiter on WFIL-TV. Following one or two brief questions, Reed lived up to his unorthodox behavior causing Keiter to become quite flustered.

"He snatched the microphone out of my hand," Keiter lamented later. "I had another question to ask but he wouldn't give the microphone back."

"I hadn't won a tournament in so long that I didn't have much to say," Reed explained. "Keiter wouldn't stop the interview so I did."

With the cameras recording this little drama, Keiter forcibly retrieved the microphone and signed off. Reed stood at his side displaying a silly grin but not saying another word.

Keiter later said, "Who says everyone is anxious to be interviewed on television?"

The Philadelphia Inquirer, February 13, 1964

there was not a ticket available. I casually mentioned that the only available seat was next to me in the broadcast booth, but that it was for my personal scorekeeper/statistician. Eddie was so desperate he asked if he could serve as my scorekeeper/statistician. I said yes and the deal was struck. He did a credible job, and I guess I did, too, since he later hired me to cover four championship fights for TVS, including Bob Foster vs. Vicente Rondon (April 7, 1972), and Joe Frazier vs. Ron Stander (May 26, 1972).

Philadelphia is indeed the personification of a great sports town, but if someone were to ask me what the *heart* of the Philadelphia experience was for me, over all of the nearly ten years spent there, I would automatically respond: "Big Five college basketball." The era of Big Five basketball put Philadelphia in the national spotlight and was a highlight of my career. The Big Five rivalry was one of the most colorful stories in all of college sports, especially the era from the early 1950s through the · 1960s. The Big Five are La Salle, Villanova, Temple, St. Joseph's and the University of Pennsylvania. While I was in Philadelphia, each of the schools had an outstanding basketball program. The excitement generated at games played between two of the Big Five schools was unparalleled.

After years of WFIL Radio coverage, we signed a contract with the Big Five to do television broadcasts of the inter-school games. I wound up doing about six games a week and most nights were double-headers. All the games were played in the beloved and hallowed halls of the Palestra. The 10,000-seat Palestra was hot, old-fashioned, perfect—and packed on Big Five basketball nights. Few tickets were available for the general public because the students, the players' families, and alumni had first crack at the rooting sections across the floor from each other. Season ticket holders took the remaining seats. The season-long battle for the city title was fearsome. The hometown contests were in addition to the games each of the five schools played in their own conferences or independent basketball schedules. But it was the games between the schools that generated city-wide excitement and emotion.

The phenomenon of the Big Five, with its consistently high level of play, brought some of the top schools in the country to play in Philadelphia. Legendary coach Adolph Rupp brought his Kentucky Wildcats to play. Dean Smith brought North Carolina. Duke, Stanford, Notre Dame, and a host of other top teams seemed to be in Philadelphia almost nightly to take on one of the Big Five. This marvelous basketball action was capped each year by the NCAA pre-regional games that were held in the Palestra.

The University of Pennsylvania Quakers were members of the Ivy League. In fact they were more successful in the Ivy League than they were against Big Five opponents. Penn won its share of Ivy League championships, but as I look back, I think they only won one Big Five title while I was involved in broadcasting Big Five games. St. Joseph's turned out many great players through the years. St. Joseph's played a hard-nosed, aggressive style of basketball, typical of the city's personality. La Salle had an excellent basketball team, winning several Big Five championships while I was there. They were a national powerhouse. In 1954 they won the NCAA Division I Championship with the great All-American player Tom Gola. Villanova, NCAA Division I champs in 1985, and Temple were probably the two most consistent members of the Big Five, and they have remained NCAA powerhouses season after season.

But back then, the city was caught up in a dramatic excitement that I have never seen in basketball anywhere else. You could sense the rivalries between the schools when you walked into the Palestra. It was palpable. The schools were located fairly close together but had little to do with each other—until the night of a game. Then they would all converge on the Palestra, which was right in the middle of the University of Pennsylvania campus. Fans couldn't park anywhere near the Palestra, so there were streams of foot traffic heading for the night's game. It was like a block party with good-natured barbs and taunts being thrown back and forth. There was a lot of screaming and yelling but very few confrontations. Students and fans were more interested in seeing exciting basketball. All this took place at least two or three nights a week all the way through the hoop season.

The enthusiasm of the fans was extreme at times, like the afternoon I was to speak at a pep rally at St. Joseph's. I was detained by my duties at the station and had to cancel at the last minute. But the St. Joe's students weren't going to hear of it. They streamed out of their gymnasium, onto the city streets, and marched across town to the WFIL television studios, chanting "WE WANT LES! WE WANT LES!" When they arrived, still chanting, outside the WFIL offices, a somewhat agitated station

Book 'em, Danno!

About 100 St. Joseph's College basketball enthusiasts showed up at City Hall singing "When the Hawks Go Marching In," and chanting "Go Hawks—Go, Go, Go!"

Somebody called the cops and the Bird Lovers went . . . straight to jail.

It all started yesterday, when the rowdy students, overjoyed by their team's gaudy 24 and 1 record and a berth in the NCAA tournament, stormed into the WFIL-TV studios on City Line ave. and demanded to see Les Keiter, their favorite sportscaster. (This is the second time the St. Joseph's students have attempted to serenade Keiter.)

Keiter, who broadcasts all Big Five games, was out tracking down ring-tailed howitzers or something. But it didn't keep the celebrants from holding a full scale peprally in the studio lobby—until their spirit was spirited outside by studio guards.

Undaunted, the rooters jumped into cars and motored to City Hall where drivers zipped their cars right smack into the center of the courtyard scattering shoppers and startling city brass.

Four floors above, participants in a murder trial could hardly hear testimony when clamor of the mob's drums, air horns, songs, cheers and clashing together of trash can lids reached the courtroom.

In a second-floor courtroom, proceedings temporarily ground to a halt while the presiding judge went to the window then explained the clatter to the jury.

Cops nabbed 29 budding Spike Joneses and led them to the 11th and Winter Streets police station where they were lectured by Capt. Anthony Wong and their dean of men, Rev. Joseph Geib.

The eight drivers had their spirits dampened even more when each were given $10 tickets for driving on the sidewalk.

Philadelphia Daily News, March 2, 1965

manager sent me outside to give the students whatever they wanted. Of course, all they wanted was a pep rally, and that's exactly what they got—right smack in front of the station. It was a tribute to their support of their team and one heck of a compliment to me.

Big Five basketball was a city success story, and the entire community was behind it. Part of the reason was the constant parade of Philadelphia high-school players who moved on to the Big Five. During the time I was there, the top high-school players seldom left the area. They wanted to play Big Five basketball. The Big Five coaches were, and indeed are still, very close to the city high-school coaches and have always recruited heavily from the Philadelphia high schools. Because of the talent emerging from the Philadelphia high schools, it was rare to hear of a player coming from outside Philadelphia to play college basketball in one of these schools. From city parks, high school, and college, the players came up through the ranks, creating an aggressive, street-smart style of play that is a trademark of Philly hoopsters. (One of the most famous Philadelphia high-school players, though, elected to play elsewhere: Wilt Chamberlain went to Kansas.) Of course, as the players moved along, they brought their families, friends, and fans, which explains some of the Big Five-mania.

And oh, how they played! Back in the 1960s there were times when four of the five schools were in the NCAA playoffs. I recall broadcasting four different Big Five schools' playoff games one season. The whole scene was amazing, and tremendous coaching was part of the reason—coaches who today form the bulwark of the NBA.

Jack McCloskey was the head coach at the University of Pennsylvania during most of my years in Philadelphia. Today Jack is the very successful general manager of the Detroit Pistons. He is the architect of the 1989 and 1990 NBA World Champions, upsetting the favored Los Angeles Lakers and then beating Portland. Prior to Detroit, Jack coached the Portland Trailblazers, and his successor there would be another 1960s Big Five alumnus, St. Joseph's coach Jack Ramsay. Under Ramsay, St. Joseph's finished in the AP Top Twenty poll three times. Their best year was 1965, ending the regular season with a 25–1 record. Dick Harter, an assistant coach under McCloskey at Penn, later got the top job and became one of the new head coaches in the NBA, after assisting Jack Ramsay with the Indiana Pacers. Dick was the first head coach of the NBA expansion team, the Charlotte Hornets. Digger Phelps, the longtime coach of Notre Dame is still another Big Five product; he was a freshman coach at Pennsylvania.

St. Joseph's had a number of fine players who went on to become successful coaches. Jim Boyle, who coached at St. Joseph's through 1989, was one of the great power forwards at the school when I was broadcasting the Big Five games. Jimmy Lynam, presently coaching the Philadelphia 76ers, succeeded Matty Guokas, Jr., another dynamic team player from St. Joseph's. Matty's father, Matt Guokas, Sr., was my first analyst and co-broadcaster when WFIL started the 76ers broadcasts. Matty Jr. went on to become head coach of the NBA Orlando Magic.

St. Joseph's Jack McKinney went on to be head coach of the Los Angeles Lakers. Unfortunately, a serious bicycle accident left him with a career-shortening concussion. He was succeeded by Paul Westhead, formerly of—you guessed it, another Big Five team—La Salle. Westhead, after coaching Loyola Marymount (led by Philadelphians Hank Gathers and Bo Kimble), another powerhouse NCAA team, went on to head up the run-and-gun Denver Nuggets. McKinney eventually recovered from the biking accident and subsequently became the head coach of the Indiana Pacers. If you get into the ranks of trainers and assistant coaches, you'll find even more connections. There's a continuous mix of ex-Big Five coaches moving throughout the NCAA and NBA.

There were other coaches who never went pro but nevertheless distinguished themselves. Villanova Wildcats' Jack Kraft, whose family became very close to ours while we lived in Philadelphia, was a highly successful coach who almost won the 1971 NCAA title. Jack's team lost to UCLA in the final and subsequently, following an NCAA investigation, had to forfeit the game due to the use of an ineligible player. It was a title he deserved and a turn of events he did not. Jack went on to coach at the University of Rhode Island and was succeeded at Villanova by Rollie Massimino. The great Harry Litwack was Temple's only coach during those years and many that followed before his retirement. Temple is still doing very well in the NCAA, a tribute to his work there.

The Big Five also had many outstanding players. I've already mentioned Matty Guokas and Jim Boyle. Jim Williams, Larry Cannon, and All-Americans Tom Gola and Paul Arizin also come to mind. Wally Jones and Jim Washington thrilled Villanova fans and the entire city during their playing days. Frank Corace of La Salle was a major reason for their success during the 1960s. Sid Amira of Pennsylvania and Guy Rodgers and Hal Lear of Temple made for exciting basketball watching when their teams were in the Palestra. There were so many more, each an important part of such noteworthy teams, that it's impossible to make a definitive list. It would be endless.

The Palestra was always packed, crammed with students and families. It was old but wore its age well. To those of us who attended basketball games in the Palestra there was something almost reverent about the place. Although it wasn't well-designed for comfortable basketball viewing, it was still fun to attend games there. Two giant scoreboards capped each end of the building. The players had to enter the court from the locker rooms underneath the stands, at which point the appropriate side would rise up to greet their team. The cheers would resound with each team's fans trying to out-cheer the other side. The noise was absolutely deafening. I can still hear the fans. It was unlike any other building in which I'd broadcast sports. And I've been in many of the college buildings where basketball is played. Today, college basketball is played in some very impressive buildings. Places such as the Spectrum in Philadelphia, the Convocation Center on Notre Dame's campus, Louisville's Freedom Hall, North Carolina's Dean Smith Center, Pauley Pavilion at UCLA, and New Mexico's "Pit" in Albuquerque are all fabulous places to watch basketball, but the Palestra, as I say, is a hallowed hall.

I had occasion to return to Philadelphia in January 1988. I was invited back for a Big Five Hall of Fame induction ceremony. In addition to the luncheon at which I was the guest speaker, I was escorted onto the floor of the Palestra to be honored in front of a packed house. The building had been painted to brighten the dark interior, but it was still full of familiar echoes. Although my return was almost twenty years after I left Philadelphia, the memories were still strong. The college students who used to attend the games were now adults with their youngsters in tow. Many came up for autographs, to shake hands, and to introduce their children to me. The legacy is being passed on. The next generation of Philadelphia basketball fans is about to catch Big Five fever.

I received another pleasant surprise during my 1988 visit.

I was the guest speaker at the 1988 Big Five Hall of Fame induction ceremony. Bob Vetrone, co-director of the Big Five, is to my left.

I was tickled to hear many of my pet broadcasting phrases still being bandied around sports circles in the city. "Keiterisms" seemed to be on the lips of every other fan I ran into. Sometimes fans just called them out by way of greeting. "In-Again-Out-Again-Finnegan!" someone would call out, and I'd wave.

It's funny how the catch phrases live on. At the awards ceremony, sportscaster Al Meltzer recalled some of my phrases when he introduced me. "Les was fun to listen to," Al told the audience. "He had phrases that I never heard before or since! I haven't the slightest idea what a 'ring-tailed howitzer' is, [but] it became part of the language of this city for a long, long time."

I suppose that today, young sportscasters must try for years to come up with a trademark phrase. For those of us who started in radio, it was really just a matter of time. You simply had to do so much more talking—and so much more description—that eventually you would repeat words that seemed to fit the bill.

I have no idea where radio broadcasters came up with their oft-repeated phrases . . . they just sort of happened. "How 'bout that?" was classic Mel Allen. "Holy Cow!" is pure Phil Rizzuto.

My favorite phrase ever was San Franciscan Jack McDonald's term for a home run: "Out Aunt Maggie's window!"

Here is a brief dictionary of basketball Keiterisms fans have not forgotten:

"Tickling the twine." That's a basket where the ball doesn't even touch the rim, just swishes the net. I don't know when I launched the term, but it was a staple all through the Big Five years.

"Ring-tailed howitzer." That's an off-balance shot that a player gets off at the last possible second as he falls. Of course it is. What else could it be?

"In-Again-Out-Again-Finnegan." Anyone knows that. It's a ball that rolls around the hoop a few times and then pops out again. Simple.

"Let's check the arithmetic!" The score, the stats, whatever.

"It's in the air . . . it's in the basket!" A good example of a phrase with radio roots. When you had the time to get a sentence like that off, everyone knew without being told that it was a thirty-footer.

"There's a lid on the bucket tonight!" A low-scoring game.

"Welcome to Panicsville, USA!" That was my traditional sign-on for Big Five games at the Palestra. It was self-explanatory, and said with great affection. The games there were as exciting as basketball gets.

Inevitably at a gathering such as the Big Five Awards Banquet, or any other time I run into an old Philadelphia fan, someone will say, "Hey, remember the Bomb Scare?" Not *a* bomb scare. *The* Bomb Scare. How could I forget? It's a great story, an incident that happened during a televised game between St. Joseph's and Villanova, one of the biggest rivalries in Big Five, with me, as always, at the microphone.

It was a cold, snowy February night. I was in my television broadcast position high above the Palestra floor, literally in the rafters. To get to our broadcast position, the crew had to climb up a long stairway and then up several sets of ladders. We had to use binoculars to identify players because the floor was so far beneath us.

It was halftime with St. Joseph's leading 30–26. I had just read the first-half statistics when several dozen uniformed men gathered on the playing floor. It seemed as if they had come from the locker rooms. And then, without any warning, a bomb squad appeared and began cutting through the crowd. At the time, of course, I could only guess who they were since we had been told nothing.

Almost simultaneously with their arrival, Mike Morgan, the courtside public address announcer and a St. Joseph's student, took the microphone and started repeating in a calm voice, "Will everybody please rise, take your coats, and leave the building?" That's all he said. It was eerie, sitting there with more than nine thousand fans watching a game, when with no warning, uniformed officers appear and everyone is asked to leave. The public address announcer just kept repeating "Will everybody please rise, take your coats, and leave the building?" And just as if someone had snapped their fingers, everyone got up and left the building. Nine thousand people filed out quietly. No one asked questions; they just put their coats on, left their briefcases and handbags, and calmly exited the building.

From my vantage point I could also see the two teams running up the steps and out of the building, so I made some remark to the effect that obviously something was wrong. (I don't miss a thing, do I?) But since the the whole affair was being televised live, I had to keep on broadcasting. The police were searching the briefcases that had been left behind. They were looking through the empty stands as the last people were going out the door, glancing over their shoulders and wondering what was happening. I reported it all. No one had given us a shred of information, so I had my statistician, Toby DeLuca, call down to the Palestra offices and try to obtain some official information as to why the building had been evacuated. I kept speculating on the air, trying to guess what was going on. It wasn't great journalism, but it was terrific theater.

What were our cameras showing all this time? The cameras were panning the stands, showing the officers looking under seats, in briefcases, and searching the building's non-seating areas. I continued to describe each scene as it came up on the monitor. Suddenly, there was a shot of the chief police officer, the head man, as he discovered us up in the rafters. He pointed at us, ordering us to vacate the building, shouting, "Anyone still in the building, any officials . . . out! Everyone out!" I was looking at the screen at this big police officer, pointing up at me and screaming, "You guys out! Get off that stand and out of the building." So I announced that we had been ordered out of the building and would be sending our broadcast back to the studio. The only assumption I could make was that it was a bomb scare. "Get out of here or I am going to go up there and get you!" yelled the officer as the cameras continued to capture the action. I didn't know what to do. So I again announced that we had been ordered out of the building and began to sign off. I was still signing off when the phone rang. Toby answered it.

It was Tom Jones, our program director. "Toby, tell Les he is not going anywhere. Stay on the air. What you're doing is beautiful. Everybody in Philadelphia is tuning to our channel. This is the biggest story that we've had in months, so no matter what happens, stay on the air until I give you further notice."

Armed with fresh orders, I told our audience, "Correction. We are not going off the air. We are staying on the air to describe events as they unfold."

When it became clear to the officer that we weren't going to leave, all of Philadelphia could see that he was wild with rage. He turned to a couple of big, burly police officers and ordered them to remove us, with force if necessary. By the time those two officers reached our broadcast position, our cameraman had piled some heavy equipment on the top of the ladder leading to the broadcast booth so they couldn't get to us. We were safely barricaded in. Safe from the police, that is, not the bomb. There was no way they could get us off the air, so I made some light comment saying, "The only way you'll see me leaving is through the building if the bomb goes off. Toby and I will go right through the ceiling."

Even though I said it with humor, the remark caused a great deal of consternation because there was a growing fear among viewers who had friends or family members at the game, although by that time, most of them were outside the Palestra, standing in the snow. The whole city was tuned to our station. Everybody started calling everyone else: "Quick, turn to Channel Six; a bomb is going to go off, live! Les Keiter is about to get blown through the Palestra!" Our ratings must have hit a zillion.

The police found no evidence of a bomb, so eventually the angry officer said that the fans could come back in again. With one last ugly glance at me, he departed with his troops. I silently hoped he wouldn't be waiting for me after the game. The crowd returned. And finally, the teams came running back onto the court. The players had gone to a gym in another building to practice and keep warm. In retrospect, the whole thing is pretty funny, and to this day, people still ask me to tell this story. It may seem strange to say it, but bomb scares, like so many things from the turbulent 1960s, are a source of nostalgia.

I have a plaque somewhere that the Philadelphia city council gave me for my courage. Courage? I had no choice—I was told what to do! To me, Mike Morgan, the P.A. announcer, was the real hero. He never raised his voice. He could have panicked everyone, but he dealt with it so beautifully that everyone calmly filed out. He too was honored by the city for his courage and level-headedness in the handling of the crowd. Ironically, the game became secondary. I can't even remember who won. The bomb scare was definitely the main event that night.

Unfortunately, the Big Five itself has lost much of its glamour and competition. The rivalry among the schools doesn't seem as intense today as it was in the 1960s. A couple of the schools, Villanova and Temple, now play games in their own gyms. I heard that La Salle moved back to Convention Hall. Some Big Five games are played at the Spectrum, where the NBA 76ers play. Competitively, Temple, Villanova, and La Salle have prevailed in recent years, while St. Joe's and Pennsylvania

Not Quite the Way Les Remembers

As an audience of 10,000 fled a bomb scare in the Palestra, WFIL-TV sports director Les Keiter gave viewers a terrifying half-hour of unscheduled drama. Les stuck with the Police and Fire Department team scouring the building, after an anonymous call emptied it between halves of the St. Joseph's-Villanova basketball game February 20.

Ignoring all personal danger, the famed sportscaster provided the tri-state video audience with the most detailed, tense closeup of a bomb hunt ever seen on the home screen. Thousands of congratulatory letters have poured into the Keiter office in the ensuing few days.

Triangle Publications News Release,
February 26, 1965

have been less triumphant. All still have solid sports programs, though, that are no doubt a continuing source of pride for many Philadelphia fans.

For me there was nothing to match the heat and competition produced by the games played from 1963 to 1970, truly a thrilling time. And no place will ever produce such a magical experience for me as the famed Palestra. It remains a shrine to the many great games it has seen, and echoes with the voices of the countless players, coaches, and fans who have filled its drafty interior. I'm proud to be one of those voices, those echoes, that haunt that lovely old arena.

My Brief Career as an
NBA Manager

And playing hardball with Walter Annenberg

As I'VE SAID, Philadelphia is one of *the* great sports communities in America. But shortly before my arrival there, the Philadelphia Warriors of the National Basketball Association moved their franchise to San Francisco (and in time became the Golden State Warriors), leaving the Philadelphia fans without a professional basketball team. The absence of a professional basketball team is not, perhaps, the greatest tragedy Philadelphia has experienced, but it was a significant loss nonetheless. However, it couldn't last for long, and it didn't. After a one-year hiatus, Philadelphia businessman Irv Kosloff and attorney Ike Richman (lawyer for Warrior star Wilt Chamberlain) purchased the Syracuse Nationals (nicknamed the "Nats") from owner Dan Biasone. The team was going to relocate from Syracuse to Philadelphia.

The next day the news of the purchase appeared on the AP and UPI news service wires. The very alert sports director of WFIL (yours truly), who had heard rumors of the impending deal, quickly tracked down station program director Tom Jones at his home. I said, "Tom, let's make a deal with this new NBA team before another station grabs them! All the rights—television and radio!"

Tom quickly agreed: "Let's do it. I'll get the go-ahead from George and Roger." George Koehler was WFIL general manager and Roger Clipp was executive manager. Both reported to the man who owned it all—radio, television, the *Philadelphia Daily News* and the famous *The Philadelphia Inquirer*—Mr. Walter Annenberg, advisor to senators, presidents and (presumably) kings.

A breakfast meeting between the new club officials and WFIL was arranged for the following Sunday morning at the Marriott Hotel, across from our studios on City Line Avenue. Nearby were the NBC and CBS affiliate stations which I knew also wanted the broadcast rights to the team. Wrapping up an agreement at this meeting was a necessity if we wanted to preempt the other stations from entering into negotiations with the new owners. Breakfast began at ten o'clock, and before we left the table we had negotiated a three-year deal. WFIL would broadcast all games on the radio and a limited schedule of live television broadcasts. The agreement was a terrific coup for WFIL. Starting with the 1963–64 season, Philadelphia had an NBA team again and WFIL had the privilege of bringing the games to the fans.

Dolph Schayes was the team's coach. The players roster read like the Who's Who of the NBA of a decade later: Larry Costello (who would coach the Milwaukee Bucks), the big redhead Johnny Kerr (now the voice of the Chicago Bulls), and Al Bianchi (who would become general manager of the New York Knicks). Other team members included Paul Neumann, Hal Greer, Dave Gambee, and Connie Dierking. There were, however, some problems to overcome.

First of all, the team had no name. The "Nats" had no local significance; besides, it was well-recognized by all concerned that the team needed to shed the "outsider" image. A contest was held to name the team. The contest drew thousands of entries, and the winning name was perfect: the Syracuse Nationals became the Philadelphia 76ers.

The season began with a game in Detroit. The players looked resplendent in their red, white, and blue uniforms. Co-owners Ike Richman and Irv Kosloff flew in to appear with me at halftime, and a new chapter began in Philadelphia sports history: the era of the Sixers. (It was an inauspicious beginning—we lost.)

Home games were played in Convention Hall, so named because of the many Democratic and GOP national conventions the building had hosted over preceding decades. It had witnessed a lot of American history, but the building was another obstacle to success for the new team. Convention Hall had certainly seen better days. It was old.

But the biggest problem had to do with the team's continuing reputation with fans as interlopers—the Syracuse Nats dressed up in 76ers uniforms. And of course the Philadelphia crowds missed Wilt Chamberlain and the Warriors. The fans just couldn't bring themselves to adopt the new team. And speaking of crowds, we weren't getting any. Attendance was so sparse it was embarrassing. A typical game would draw only fifteen hundred to seventeen hundred spectators.

It was no surprise then, when on one of the chartered flights to do TV coverage of a road game Mr. Kosloff and Mr. Richman, the proud new owners of the Philadelphia 76ers, came forward and asked, "Les, what's the matter with this city? We've spent a lot of money to bring this team here. People should be *flocking* to Convention Hall! The apathy is astounding—the people just aren't behind the team!" Of course, it was terribly ironic that they would ask *me* about "this city." I had only been in town a year or so—they both went back a lot further in Philadelphia than I did!

But since they asked, I told them, "You've got two problems. First, you need some local players." The Big Five was at its crest. Just a few blocks from Convention Hall stood the Palestra, where nearly ten thousand people were pouring in on Tuesday, Thursday, and Saturday nights to watch the college doubleheaders. You couldn't get tickets for the place, the hotbed of eastern basketball! Meanwhile, the pro team in town was having trouble getting over a thousand paying fans into Convention Hall, and *bored* fans at that. "If you want to get the Palestra-type crowds in to watch the 76ers, you need to get some Big Five players onto the team. Draft a couple of them, like Wally Jones from Villanova, or Matty Guokas from St. Joseph's." (Jones would go on to become a star with the Sixers, and Matty Guokas would later coach the team to NBA success, but I won't pretend that I was knowingly so prophetic.)

"And your other problem," I continued, "is the two of you gentlemen. One of you owns a paper company," as Irv Kosloff still does, "and Ike, you're an attorney. You're both great successes, experts in your fields. But basketball is not your field. Back off. Hire a general manager to run your team, someone who knows the NBA. You need a guy who can talk authoritatively with Ned Irish of the Knicks, Red Auerbach of the Celtics, and Ben Kerner of the St. Louis Hawks. Otherwise, you're going to get snookered in any deal with another organization, because they've got people who know their way around the league. Neither of you has that kind of experience. Let someone else handle the day-to-day running of the club. Then you can stay home and run your businesses and enjoy being the owners of a professional basketball team." And that was the end of the conversation. Or so I thought at the time.

Weeks passed and the situation remained pretty much the same. People were, as the saying goes, staying away in droves; there was just no support at all. I traveled with the team when it was on the road. When we were at home, I'd do my six o'clock television sportscast, run to the Convention Center to broadcast the 76ers game and then rush back to the station to prepare for the late news sportscast. It was a crazy schedule, but I was young and energetic and most of all, I was really excited about the Sixers. It was a promising team, and I was disturbed that such a great town as Philadelphia was so blatantly ignoring them.

Then, one night as I walked into Convention Hall, Irv Kosloff was waiting for me. Brief greetings were exchanged, and then he took me under the grandstand—very mysterious and clandestine. "Do you remember the conversation we had with Ike on the plane a few weeks ago?" he asked. "About the two problems you said we had. Well, we've talked it over, we've decided you're right, and we're going to do what you suggested."

"Terrific!" I said, "You're going to draft Wally Jones and Matt Guokas."

"Well, yes, we're thinking about that, too. But we're definitely going to do the other thing," he replied.

"About hiring a basketball man to run this team?"

"Right. We've even decided who it's going to be."

"Beautiful!"

Irv looked me in the eyes. "It's you!" he said.

I was flabbergasted. "What do you mean ME??!!"

"We're going to hire you. You're going to be our general manager."

I just laughed at him. "Hey, I'm just a TV and radio sportscaster, I'm not an NBA general manager."

"You'd be a natural. We checked with some people in the NBA, and they all said you passed the inspection. You know the game, and we'll pay you a lot more money to be general manager of the 76ers than you'll ever get in sportscasting. We want you to start immediately!"

I said, "I've got a contract with Triangle Productions. And that's Walter Annenberg!" What a scene! I had to go on the air in about twelve minutes, and there I was standing under the bleachers in Convention Hall with Irv Kosloff saying, "You're going to be the GM of a professional basketball team." His offer was from out of left field; it simply had never occurred to me. I needed to sit down and talk to my family. Did we want to go into basketball instead of this career I had been pursuing all of my life? I had to meet with people at work because I had a written contract. I said, "We'll talk later."

Then as we walked toward the broadcast table, I added, "I tell you what you should do, Kos. Call Tom Jones at Channel Six and tell him that you want to talk to me. Otherwise, it's like tampering with a player from another team. If a player is under contract, you've got to ask the owner for permission to talk to him. Talk to Tom Jones. Tell him you want to meet with me, and then we'll all sit and we'll talk . . . *after* I do the game."

Irv wouldn't give it up. "Is he working tonight?" I said, "He's always at the station at night; he's a workaholic." Tom Jones was not only a workaholic but also a sportsaholic. He had put the Washington Redskins network together and loved everything about sports and sports broadcasting.

"Great!" I really had to get going. "See you later!"

I headed straight to the booth and got to work, doing the radio broadcast of the game. I would learn later that Irv headed straight to the Convention Hall office, shut the door, called Channel Six and asked for Tom Jones. "Tom, it's Kos." Now, understand that Irv is something of a jokester—a real kidder. So instead of saying to Tom, "I need to talk with you about Les," or "We're interested in hiring Les for the 76ers," he said "We're going to steal Keiter from you."

"What are you talking about, Irv?" asked Jones.

"Keiter's going to be our general manager—we've already talked to him, and we're going to steal him from WFIL."

Well, Tom wasn't sure what in the world was going on, so he sort of laughed and told Kosloff he and the station brass would be in touch. Then he hung up the phone and ran downstairs to his boss George Koehler and told him the story. Koehler couldn't believe it. "That's what Irv said," Tom repeated, " 'We're going to steal Keiter!' "

"They can't do that," said George. "Keiter's under contract! We'll stop him!" He called Triangle head man Roger Clipp and related the incident to him. Now Roger Clipp wasn't a warm guy at all; he was very businesslike and a little on the mean side. He wasted no time in his reaction: he went directly to Walter Annenberg.

I had only met Mr. Annenberg once. But he was known by all of us as the absolute ruler of his empire. He was not only total in his power; he was also, as I was about to learn, very vindictive.

The next morning Annenberg, as owner of the *Philadelphia Daily News*, ordered writer Jack Kiser to quit writing feature stories on the 76ers. He was told he would no longer be traveling with the team. Annenberg also wrote an internal memo to both of his newspapers, the *Philadelphia Daily News* and *The Philadelphia Inquirer*, stating that all stories about the 76ers' games were to appear on inside pages. The stories would be cut to two paragraphs if the team won, three if they lost. I was told no longer to mention the Sixers on my daily radio show or television sportscast except to say, "The 76ers play the Pistons tonight at Convention Hall," on the six o'clock newscast and the final score of the game on the late newscast. That's all. There would be no additional coverage of the team, no more features, no ads—Annenberg cancelled everything, effective immediately. We did have a contract for radio play-by-play of their games, and we would continue, but there would be no promotion of upcoming broadcasts. And Annenberg said he planned to cancel both the television and the radio agreements with the 76ers because they had "violated their contract" by trying to "steal his announcer."

I was warned by station executives Jones and Koehler, "Don't discuss this again with anybody. Don't talk to Kosloff or Richman about the job!" I had already discussed the job with Lila and we had decided to turn it down. The position offered no real security—the longevity of a general manager in the NBA was very limited. But the threats and hassles from Annenberg and company made me want to say, "To hell with Channel Six!" and take the job. But the moment passed, and despite Jones and Koehlers' warning I called Kosloff and Richman and told them that I wasn't interested.

"But, what if we doubled your pay?"

"Not interested. Sorry. Thank you." But the damage had been done.

Suddenly there was no writer with the team. The team couldn't get into the columns. I had to tell the owners and players that there wouldn't be any columns at all. Or radio features. Or television. Once it became apparent to the 76ers that Annenberg was doing serious damage to the team, Kosloff asked me to arrange a meeting for them with Walter Annenberg to see how to stop this. "This is ridiculous!" he said, "Annenberg can't do that to us!" In fact, he could, and he had. I sent word up through channels that 76ers owners Mr. Richman and Mr. Kosloff would like a meeting with Mr. Annenberg to discuss the current problem between Mr. Annenberg and the 76ers. Tom Jones took the request to Annenberg, who replied, "Who?! I don't know them."

Tom Jones tried to explain, "But they want to—"

"Don't ever mention them to me again. I don't want to hear the names Kosloff or Richman again in my company, or none of you will have jobs here." That's how vindictive he was. There would be no meetings, no appeals, no discussion. Period.

Of course, I became the man in the middle. Irv was screaming at me, and Ike was screaming at me. Several days had gone by, and hardly a word appeared in the paper. Attendance at 76ers games dropped from fifteen hundred to five hundred because no one knew there was a game on. There were no promotions. No announcements. Nothing. And other stations weren't plugging the team because the games were on our station. It was as if the 76ers had dropped off the face of the earth.

Word had reached the rest of the NBA. They were becoming concerned about the low attendance and lack of media coverage. I received calls from Ned Irish in New York and a day later from Ben Kerner in St. Louis: "Les, what's going on? Is there a boycott? Our teams are coming into Philadelphia, and no one's showing up for the games! Get that damn Annenberg off our backs!" Everyone with the team and the whole of the NBA was pushing me to fix things, and everyone in my own organization was telling me to shut up, not do anything, walk away, and follow Annenberg's orders. What a nightmare! What would happen next? The situation couldn't get any worse.

It did.

At a sports banquet at the B'nai B'rith I was cornered by

Phillies manager John Quinn, Eagles coach Joe Kuharich, and Sixers coach Dolph Schayes. All of the Philadelphia sports teams were concerned about Annenberg's actions. I sensed they felt that any sport I covered would be affected by the Annenberg boycott. As one voice they said, "You've got to do something and do it fast. Otherwise you'll never announce another pro sport in this town!" No real threats were intended, of course, but tempers had flared to a flash point. Annenberg felt it, too. Kosloff told me later that a close, mutual friend of Annenberg and mine had tried to reason with Annenberg about the situation and that Annenberg had thrown the friend—a good friend—right out of his office. Everyone was angry.

The boycott continued for nearly two months, and it was based on a ridiculous half-joking comment made by Irv Kosloff.

Then, as suddenly as it began, it ended. Word came down from Annenberg's office that Jack Kiser could begin covering the team and writing features. Radio and television reporting was reinstated, and we could promote our play-by-play coverage. No explanations, no apologies, and no comments were made, nor would they ever be made. Mr. Annenberg had satisfied his own anger and had lifted the boycott.

The 76ers continued to feel the boycott's impact through the rest of the season. Recovery from that disastrous first year was slow but would follow with the hiring of a great general manager, Jack Ramsay, and the acquisition of some Big Five players. And finally, when Eagles owner Jerry Wolman built the Spectrum, the Sixers escaped the inappropriate Convention Hall. I thought that I had escaped relatively unscathed from the incident. I never had another such encounter with Mr. Annenberg.

But as recently as 1989, I heard a story from Philadelphia sportswriter Frank Dolson. He asked if I remembered the stories that President Richard Nixon had compiled an "Enemies List" during the Watergate era. Apparently Nixon had borrowed the idea of such blackballing from his close, personal friend Walter Annenberg, who kept his own "Enemies List." Frank told me that one of the names on Annenberg's list was Les Keiter.

If an Annenberg "Enemies List" existed, and if I was indeed on it, I will never know if it had any effect on my career in Philadelphia or elsewhere. But judging from the vindictive nature of Walter Annenberg, I can only assume that inclusion on such a list must have put me in some pretty good company.

A Night in Miami

Sonny and Cassius, with Keiter at ringside

CLAY VS. LISTON, 1964. Miami Beach. Their first fight. The birth of a new era in professional boxing, and indeed, in the American sports scene.

I put aside my day-to-day duties as sports director of WFIL Philadelphia to perform the Clay-Liston blow-by-blow honors for ABC Radio. This bout was one of eight heavyweight championship fights I would do for ABC. My color commentator for each bout was Howard Cosell. I had been fortunate to have called some spectacular championship fights to date—the three Patterson-Johansson matchups come to mind—but this fight looked to be something unique, and I was delighted to be invited ringside to describe the action for ABC Radio and for a closed-circuit viewing audience. Clay and Liston, so different from one another, promised fireworks, and they did not disappoint.

I had first met Sonny Liston in 1961, calling my first nationally broadcast fight in a so-called "coaxial-cable doubleheader."

113

Chris Schenkel was in Toronto, calling the Floyd Patterson–Tom McNeeley heavyweight championship bout. I was in Philadelphia covering the even greater mismatch of Sonny Liston against Germany's Albert Westphal. The split-city split-bill was a buildup to an intended pairing of heavyweight champ Patterson and Liston. Liston vs. Westphal was the first national presentation of Liston, who had recently been released from prison. Liston's coming-out was impressive. In what must be the shortest fight of my broadcasting career, Liston knocked out Westphal in just seventeen seconds in the first round. Westphal wasn't a true heavyweight, to be sure, but Liston looked ferocious: a huge fighter with the most powerful punches I had ever seen. Westphal was beaten before he began. Liston's savage blows would do their job again and again in the years to follow as he gained and defended the heavyweight title by destroying all comers, even great fighters like Floyd Patterson. On the eve of the Miami Beach fight with Clay, Sonny Liston was still the quintessential heavyweight fighter. In my mind, and in the minds of most boxing experts, Liston was unbeatable, unstoppable, and unmerciful.

But Cassius Clay's star was on the rise. The first time I saw him was in 1963 at the second Liston-Patterson bout held at the Las Vegas Convention Center. It was the first time the professional boxing public really had a chance to see the young fighter from Louisville. Clay had emerged on the sports scene as the boxing hero of the 1960 Olympics. He had rapidly gained a reputation as a good professional boxer and was considered a legitimate contender for the heavyweight title. And what a sight we saw that night in Las Vegas! Clay was introduced just before the main event. (It was already assumed that he would soon be matched with the winner of the fight.) Clay stepped into the ring, gave the obligatory wave to the crowd, shook hands with Patterson, crossed to the opposite corner to meet Liston, and then a dozen steps away from Sonny, stopped dead in his tracks and started taunting the champion. "I want you . . . I want to rumble with you . . . I'm going to get you, you *big ugly bear!*" Outrageous! Liston, who was never all that sharp anyway, just stared at him. No reaction at all. He didn't know what to make of this brash young kid who had the gall to goad him in front of thousands of people. Frankly, no one else knew what to make of him either. But there was young Clay, laughing, taunting, and pointing at the awesome Liston *and getting away with it!* It defied description.

Sonny Liston's unbeaten record remained intact as he knocked Patterson out in the first round. Eventually the match with Cassius Clay was set for February 25, 1964, in the Miami Beach Convention Center. I flew to Florida, got settled in my downtown Miami hotel, and soon the uniqueness of this bout began to surface. An ABC producer called me the morning of the bout and gave me a truly unusual assignment. ABC wanted to broadcast the weigh-in of the boxers at noon. Never had I been asked to broadcast a weigh-in. "Why the hell do you want to broadcast that?" I asked, "All they do is step on the scales,

Strong Hands and a Weak Tongue

One of the highlights of the electronic doubleheader was the interview by Les Keiter of heavyweight fighter Sonny Liston.

Liston had just knocked out West German Albert Westphal in one punch. Sonny stood there in the center of the ring while Keiter, full of bounce, began to throw right- and left-handed questions.

Good old Les' high-speed spewing had Liston more confused in one minute, 58 seconds than was Westphal, at that moment having his face splashed with wake-up water.

Sonny answered the first question, something about how he felt, with an "Uh-huh." The next concerned the power of his punch, and Sonny pondered a moment before grunting, "Tha's right."

A third question was a stunner. Keiter, realizing his word battle was one-sided, dwelled at some length on the manly art and then ended with something like, "Did you realize the forcefulness of your final punch was conclusive?"

Sonny reeled and blinked, then blurted, "Did I what the WHAT?"

But who needs to be glib when he owns million-dollar knuckles?

San Francisco Chronicle, December 6, 1961

the doctor checks their vital signs, and everybody leaves!"

"We think this time might be a little different" was the producer's cryptic reply. I was irritated at not being able to write my pre-fight opening remarks but went out and hailed a cab. A half-hour later my cab was going over the bridge to Miami Beach. On arrival I found an unusually huge outpouring of media and reporters—I recall the great Red Smith in the throng—all waiting for what should be a routine event.

Cassius Clay entered with a phalanx of bikini-clad girls leading his entourage. "I want to rumble! Where is that ugly bear?" The brash kid persona was still in evidence. "I can't wait for tonight, I want that ugly bear NOW!" This from a challenger facing the most powerful hitter in the history of the sport. It seemed that Clay knew no fear. Then Sonny arrived with much less fanfare, dressed in his shorts, a towel hanging around his neck. As the two stood at the podium for photos, Clay continued the taunting. "I want you now, you big ugly bear! I want to rumble with you! I'm going to be the champion!" Suddenly, Liston responded to the goading and lunged for Clay. The two were quickly pulled apart. But the crowd was buzzing about what had just taken place. The hype was on.

So their weights were taken, the boxing commission staff was writing down all the data on their clipboards, and suddenly there was another surprise. The doctor told the commissioner Clay's blood pressure was too high. Clay was told he had until four o'clock to lower his blood pressure or risk forfeiture of the match. Speculation in the press corps went rampant following the commissioner's announcement. Obviously the loud kid's bravado was only skin-deep; underneath he was as nervous as a cat. Even when he later passed the physical exam, the consensus opinion remained the same—Clay was scared to death.

I thought so too, until I returned to the arena later that evening. It was about 8:30. The preliminary bouts were underway in the darkened arena. I spotted Clay nearby—easy to recognize in an all-white suit—watching the match in progress. His younger brother Rudy was making his big-card debut in a four-round fight. Clay was following the fight like any big brother, calling out encouragement, doing a bit of shadow-boxing. He appeared to me to be the calmest guy in the world—icy calm. I suddenly realized how phony the concerns of the afternoon had been. Clay could never have really been in the state of fear and agitation assumed by most. He didn't look like he had a care in

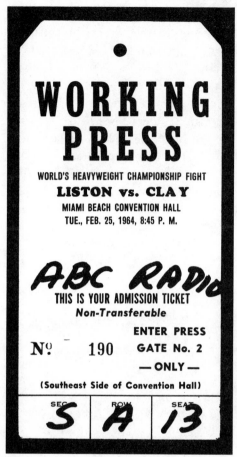

My press pass for the first Liston-Clay fight.

the world. And in my estimation, his odds to dethrone the champ jumped sharply.

Ten o'clock, and it was showtime. The opponents entered the arena and the ring. Clay's coolness remained. Liston—as always—had no expression at all, just that dull blank animal-like stare. The contrasts between the two couldn't have been more extreme.

The champion was a massive fighter, six feet, three inches tall, 240 pounds. No finesse, just raw brute strength, and as already noted, those hammering punches that could take a man's head right off. Clay was right: Liston *was* a big, ugly bear, with the meanness to match. The challenger was younger, lighter, six feet, three inches tall, 210 pounds. He had fast hands, fast feet, and he was counting on that speed to capture the heavyweight championship. It was possible he might out-box the ugly bear. The big unanswered question was "How could Clay stand up to the thunderous punching power of Sonny Liston?"

In his previous two bouts, Liston had knocked out Patterson in the first round of their first fight, and in the rematch he had Patterson on the canvas three times in the first round. He hit so hard and he was so huge, he seemed unbeatable.

Tonight would tell. Two unbeaten fighters stared at each other from opposite corners. Someone had to fall. Nothing in all of sports compares to when two men of such stature meet for a heavyweight championship fight. It's one-on-one, and it's for the most prestigious title in all of boxing. I will admit that it is my favorite moment in broadcasting.

Clay–Liston Fight: Keiter's Opening Comments

"Another boxing milestone is at hand. . . . In just a few minutes Louisville's Cassius Marcellus Clay climbs the steps into Miami Beach's 22 foot ring here at Convention Hall to face the target of his constant needle . . . to run head on into the devastating punches of the Heavyweight Boxing Champion, Sonny Liston. . . . The man who has been screaming to the heavens that he is the greatest meets his destiny . . . the awesome Sonny Liston. . . . A man cut from the mold of Joe Louis . . . A champion who rules supreme . . . Who can take a man out with either hand . . . A ring executioner who has disposed of his opposition in less than a round the last three times he has answered the bell. . . . Now as sportsdom's most electric moment draws near, despite a cloudy day here in Miami that was expected to help the live gate Convention Hall will be somewhat less than filled to its 16,000 capacity. . . . And Boxing's top experts, the more than 100 Boxing writers from all over the globe are here in Miami . . . "

Les Keiter, ABC Radio, February 25, 1964

I'm glad Sonny Liston was in a good mood when this picture was taken; look at the size of his hands!

The bell rang for Round One. Both fighters came out somewhat cautious, tentative. Liston was aggressive, but restrained. Clay danced, backpedaling, landing a few jabs that did no damage. The champion landed a few punches, too, but none of the great haymakers that had put other contenders out in the first round. Toward the end of the round, Clay put together some sharp combinations to Sonny's head, and the pace of the fight rapidly picked up. Both boxers got their adrenalin pumping, and at the closing bell, kept slugging away at each other like kids in a school yard, until the referee succeeded in getting them back to their corners.

The next round brought more of the same. Liston came out the aggressor again—it was the only way he knew how to fight—but Clay, apparently satisfied at what he learned in the previous round, exhibited the hand and foot speed that was his trademark. Clay's jabs were faster, more frequent, and they carried a good sting. Liston's head was snapping back with regularity, and Clay's feet never stopped. When Liston started throwing the big bombers, Clay just wasn't there to meet them; he was dancing around the big bear. The punches that did land caused no damage, landing on the challenger's shoulders or grazing his forehead. The round could have been called even due to Liston's aggressiveness.

But Round Three showed a different Cassius Clay. Clay came out as the aggressor, cranking himself up to full throttle. Liston couldn't touch him. For every punch Liston threw, Clay answered with a flurry of quick jabs, a feint, a dance, and yet another jab. Liston was confused. He had no answer for the speed of the Olympic champ. It was unbelievable: hands and feet and head and then something more. The taunting began again. Clay laid into Sonny with a staccato series of verbal jabs, point and counterpoint with his fists. It may have distracted Liston as much as the speed. Not only was Liston stalking a mirage that disappeared just when the punches were supposed to land, but the mirage was talking a blue streak, making fun of Liston and then landing stinging jabs on his face and arms. The champion kept plodding; the challenger kept dancing. Sonny was getting a boxing lesson from Clay.

Then Sonny got cut above the eye, and what a sobering sight it was to see the mighty Liston bleeding at the hands of this young kid! The "certain" destruction of Cassius Clay had faded in the eyes of most spectators. The unbeaten champion was getting a beating. The bell rang, and a companion at ringside, undefeated retired champion Rocky Marciano summed it up succinctly: "I never thought I would see a heavyweight Sugar Ray Robinson. I have tonight."

Clay was phenomenal at that point of the match.

Then another bizarre twist occurred after the bell sounded to start the fifth round. Clay moved to the center of the ring, then turned back to his corner, waving his gloves in front of his face, shouting "I can't see! I can't see!" Trainer Angelo Dundee, who must have acted on sheer instinct and experience, leapt onto the ring apron, spun Clay around by the waist, and *shoved* him at Liston, who was watching the entire scene with befuddlement. (Sonny presumably could have walked up behind

Clay and knocked him cold, but his wits and his corner failed him, and he did nothing.) Clay continued to shake his head, gloves in front of his face, protesting that he couldn't see. But Liston was on him, and if Clay was blind, he showed brilliant instincts, dodging, weaving, blinking, trying to focus, and dancing away. Liston took the lead and landed some telling blows, but he couldn't put Clay away. The implication was staggering to all watching the fight—Liston couldn't knock down a blind man! Two minutes into the round Clay began to regain his eyesight. By the next round he was in command of the fight once more.

Clay later claimed something was on Liston's gloves that blinded him. The allegation was never proven, but it is yet another colorful footnote in a colorful career.

The sixth round ended. We went to the commercial. Back on the air Howard Cosell went into his analysis of the round, then uttered the famous words: "There's the bell for the seventh round, back to Les Keiter . . . wait a minute . . . wait a minute! Sonny Liston is not coming out! Sonny Liston is not coming out for the seventh round. Cassius Clay is the new heavyweight champion of the world!" In the arena there was a second of stunned confusion, and then pandemonium erupted, led by Clay himself. Slumped in one corner, on his stool, was the immobile, utterly defeated Sonny Liston, claiming he had injured his shoulder. (It was another delusion of the bizarre evening: x-rays would later show no fracture, and in viewing the replay of the fight, you can see Liston clearly throwing his strongest punches in the sixth round.) As for Clay, he was leaping, stalking, marching about the ring, his taunting jeers now turned to the writers and broadcasters at ringside: "You didn't listen to me! You wouldn't believe me! I told you I was going to beat him! I showed you! Give me justice! I am the champion!! I am the King! I AM THE GREATEST!!!"

His trademark phrase was born. And the next day at the post-fight press conference, he announced his conversion to the Muslim faith and his new name, Muhammad Ali. Decades of further triumphs and controversy would follow the new champion. He would provide us with some of the most colorful fights in all of boxing. But he had shown it all in this first championship battle: the test of wills, the pre-fight drama, the little mysteries in and out of the ring, the apparent hopelessness followed by brilliant recoveries, and the tension-laden drama that seemed so much larger than a single fight.

But, Howard, Did You Hear the Answer?

Like a baby's lusty belch during the sermon, wry humor has a way of slipping into serious situations.

It happened Tuesday night during the radio broadcast of the championship fight between Sonny Liston and Cassius Clay. The former king, crippled and crownless, muttered to announcer Howard Cosell that his shoulder was broken.

"I see," said Cosell, with what sounded like a sympathetic cluck. "Now apart from the broken shoulder, were you hurt any?"

That was the night's funniest, if inadvertent line, but there was a warm-up to it. It came in the pre-fight portion of the program, when Cosell was interviewing the only man—until Tuesday—ever to defeat Liston. This was Marty Marshall, who bombed the woeful warrior 10 years ago. He recalled this near-forgotten triumph for Cosell, who now goes down as a difficult man to convince.

"But did you hurt him?" Cosell wondered.

"Well," drawled Marshall, "I broke his jaw. I think that hurt him."

This is not meant to demean the broadcast delivered by the American Broadcasting Co. (heard here on WLS). It was well handled and both color commentator Cosell and blow-by-blow reporter Les Keiter did a fine job. Indeed, a replay of the sixth-round tape showed Keiter as being amazingly on target. In that final session, Keiter made it clear that Liston was decidedly not himself and that something had gone wrong with the champion.

The audience figures show over 75,000,000 listened to the fight. ABC paid $325,000 for radio rights to Liston's first fight with Patterson, and $175,000 for the second. Liston's talent for brief encounters dipped the price on Tuesday's tilt to $115,000. The network found four sponsors but had to guarantee each a total of three commercial minutes.

Chicago Sun-Times, February 27, 1964

The next time I saw Ali fight was two years and four title defenses later, against Brian London in—naturally—London, England. I was covering the fight for Mutual Broadcasting, having parted ways with ABC Sports. Howard Cosell had decided that he didn't need a blow-by-blow partner anymore; he could do it all. There were no hard feelings. However large his ego, and stories about Howard's ego are legion, Howard's dealings with me had always been professional. It was Cosell who had gotten me my first "in" with ABC ("You want excitement? Get Keiter!" was his reported comment). ABC-TV was also covering the match in London, and Cosell would be seated almost directly across the ring from me and my broadcast partners, Van Patrick and Bill Stern.

In the pre-fight meeting at the hotel, the producer went over the game plan for the broadcast. It seemed that the president of Mutual Broadcasting would be at ringside, as would the president of our broadcast's sponsor, the Bic Pen company of Connecticut. Bic had paid Muhammad Ali a substantial fee to to endorse their product, but to capture that endorsement for our audience, it was up to one of us to get a microphone to Ali in the ring as soon as the fight ended. That was the easy part. The trick was to beat Cosell and ABC to the punch, because once Howard started his interview with Ali, it would almost certainly drag on past our scheduled sign-off time. Getting the microphone to the champ was a *priority*. How good a job we did covering the fight was secondary to this task.

The fight itself was a complete mismatch, as would be virtually all of Ali's fights between Liston in 1964 and Joe Frazier in 1971. Ali was in terrific condition, and Brian London didn't have a chance. He went down halfway through the third round, started to get up on the seven count and collapsed again for the knockout. Following the count-out, the race was on! I grabbed our microphone, climbed on top of our table, and made my way through the ropes. I looked and saw Howard and his cameraman doing the same. Ali had gone over to shake hands with London and then headed back to center ring. I fought my way through the ring crowd to the champ, but Cosell and company were making good time on their side. Howard was calling out to Ali, who saw (with some amusement?) us both coming. Finally, Cosell was near enough to extend his microphone and I knew it was do or die. I squeezed in between my competitor and my quarry and threw a hip-block into the six-foot-three

Cosell, knocking him back into his cameraman, and got the microphone to Ali.

"Another great night, champ!" I yelled above the din.

And Ali, with that trademark grin, grabbed the microphone from my hands, and right off the bat said, "In my home, the only pen we ever use is a Bic Pen!"

"Thanks, Champ!" End of interview. Mission accomplished. And a somewhat nonplussed Howard Cosell went about his task with his friend Muhammad Ali.

I would go on to cover Ali's next few fights, including Cleveland "Big Cat" Williams and WBA Champion Ernie Terrell. Then began Ali's long battle with the Selective Service and his four-year exile from professional boxing. I still remember the newly re-named champion saying to the press, "I ain't got nothin' against no [Viet] Cong!" And despite all that has been said of Cosell in his many years of broadcasting, he must be given credit for being the first and most vocal supporter of the dethroned champion throughout those turbulent years of the late sixties. It reminded me of his earlier support of the dejected Floyd Patterson, who had confined himself to his home, shades drawn, after his first of two first-round losses to Sonny Liston. Howard had gone to Patterson's house and literally opened the shades that Floyd had pulled on all the windows, helping his friend get back on his feet. Cosell's biggest sin, in my eyes, was his tendency to get too personally involved in the events and people that he covered, but cases like these—Patterson and Ali—make it easier to forgive him.

You know that little hip block that I threw on Cosell in London? Well, I'm sorry to admit it, Howard, but it felt terrific!

The Summer of '68

*Jesse Owens, Mexico City, and the
signs of the times*

IT WAS A TYPICAL day in early 1968. I was working at WFIL
television and radio in Philadelphia. I was preparing my script
for the evening newscast when the phone rang. The caller was
Frank Miller, a radio producer with Mutual Radio. His call led
to one of the most unforgettable experiences I have ever had in
broadcasting.

"Les, we'd like you to do the Summer Olympic Games from
Mexico City for us," he said. This wasn't a complete surprise.
Frank and I had talked several times over the preceding year
about various broadcasting possibilities. But the next part was
something special. "We're thinking of having Jesse Owens do the
commenting with you. Are you interested, and are you available?" Of course I was interested. After checking with WFIL and
my family, I made myself available. Jesse Owens was also
available.

Looking back, it's curious how many of my career highlights began with similarly mundane phone calls. All the fights were that way: "Sonny Liston and Cassius Clay . . . are you available?" "Yes, I'm available, let me double check with work and the family." Thank God for the telephone!

Getting ready for three weeks of broadcasting the Olympics took some homework. I spent days reading about what happened in the preceding Games, which were held in Tokyo: who would be coming back to compete, the current world records, the current world record holders, and the current contenders. It was certainly not enough to be an overnight expert, but at least I was conversant in all of the basics and some of the details. I knew Jim Ryun's times in the 1500-meter run and what Bob Beamon was expected to achieve in the long jump (though no one was ready for the kind of performance he would put on). I followed the training of the U.S. track and field team, which was working up in the mountains to prepare for Mexico City's high altitude. Track experts were saying that two of our runners, John Carlos and Tommie Smith, were expected to do very well in the sprints and relays. A young fighter named George Foreman was our heavyweight hope. The U.S. didn't stand a chance in wrestling against the Russians. Swimming and diving would produce a number of medals for the U.S. And so on. By the time I stepped off the plane in Mexico City, I had a working knowledge of the kinds of events that were about to unfold. Some things, of course, would turn out to be a complete surprise to me, to most of the country, and to the world.

It would be my first and only visit to Mexico City. It is one of the largest cities in the world and spectacular in many ways. However, I found it was impossible to overlook the widespread poverty and the huge ghettos. Mexico City was experiencing a lot of political unrest—student protests and even some shootings occurred in the weeks preceding the Olympics. We were warned by Olympics officials to be on our guard in and around the Olympic Village and the venues for the events.

We were also warned that the ineffectual U.S. black athlete boycott of the Olympics, proposed by a group of California-based black militants, might re-surface in Mexico City. Throughout early 1968 all black athletes and sympathetic white athletes were asked to forfeit Olympic participation as a demonstration against the treatment of all blacks living in the U.S. Few athletes, black or white, were willing to give up an opportunity to participate in one of the greatest sporting events held. The tension, however, was apparent, and the U.S. Olympic Committee was uneasy as the U.S. Olympic team converged on Mexico City.

The Olympic Village is an extraordinary place. Just walking around, being *in* the Olympic Village was an amazing feeling. The spirit, the warmth, the camaraderie, the great-to-be-here kind of atmosphere. I had a big plus, too: I was walking with Jesse Owens, and at the time he was the most instantly recognizable sports personage in the world. Wherever he went, people were calling "Jesse! Jesse!"

It seemed as if every Olympic athlete and Olympics follower knew of Jesse Owens. Thirty-two years after his triumph in the Berlin Olympics, athletes and fans from every country in the 1968 Olympics would come up to Jesse asking for autographs, wanting to have their picture taken with him (something I regretfully never did), wanting to touch him, to shake his hand. Jesse himself, standing in a group, was not an overly impressive-looking man. Modestly dressed, quiet, five foot, ten inches tall, glasses, balding—he looked like a banker or an insurance executive. But he was overwhelmed by hordes of humanity wherever he went. The Olympic athletes in their bright-hued warm-up jackets and jerseys would swarm all around him, asking question after question. I got the feeling they were hoping some of his great athleticism would rub off on them so they could walk away with a gold medal or four. The rest of Mutual's broadcast crew felt like caddies, just hanging around, waiting for Jesse to move on.

But there were certainly no hard feelings. Jesse Owens was one of the most charming, gracious, personable, likable human beings I have ever met. There existed in the man not a drop of conceit. When we were in the boxing arena, people would seek him out, and he would say, "Talk to Les here, *he's* the expert." When we broadcast a U.S. basketball game, the same would happen: Jesse would always defer to me. But when we were in the Olympic Village or at his hotel, by no choice of his own, it was all Jesse Owens.

Jesse and his wife, Ruth, were given a suite of rooms at the El Camino Royale Hotel. They were constantly entertaining guests, holding court, really. The rooms were filled with amateur sports figures flowing through every hour of the day and late into the night. Flowers, gifts, and letters were stacked all about, only to be covered with new ones. The homage and appreciation Jesse received never stopped, but none of it affected him. Again and again he would go out of his way to introduce me to people: "This is my friend, Les Keiter, the voice of Mutual." He took me under his wing during the Games. Jesse made me a kind of protégé, and I'll always be grateful. Of course, besides his fame, he was also the only American on both the United States Olympic Committee and the International Olympic Committee. He had worked with the Olympics virtually his entire life. If ever a man was truly in his own element, this was it, this was Jesse Owens' arena. And yet he would always defer to others around him, particularly his wife, Ruth, a quiet and lovely lady.

By the way, the rest of the Mutual crew and I were *not* at El Camino Royale. The name of the barn Mutual inadvertently put us up in is now happily forgotten. Each room came with a complimentary swarm of flies, a broken air conditioner, brown running water, sagging mattresses, and flickering lights. Unfortunately we were stuck with the rooms for the duration of the Olympics, as Mexico City was totally filled. Jesse actually came to our hotel to join us for our first production meeting. Being the gentleman that he is, he looked around with a very surprised expression but said nothing. Later, when the shock had worn off, he quietly said, "Let's meet at my place from now on."

And so the 1968 Olympic Games began. From the opening ceremony to the closing festivities, the Games were one big, colorful crazy blur. For a sportscaster, the Olympic Games were like a kid's first visit to Disneyland: all wonderful and seemingly infinite. One event began before the previous one finished; each event and each day blended into the next. Events were at sites spread all over the city, and we must have spent a fortune in taxi fares just getting from one venue to the next. The security was evident everywhere. Every time we would go to a new site, or into a different building, we would go through a checkpoint. The security guards would verify that we were displaying the proper ID card or the right badge. We felt like costume party generals walking around with all these badges and pins displayed. But given the warnings that something might happen, we were willing to put up with the inconvenience caused by the heavy security. Jesse and I were doing three live reports a day for Mutual. Every other waking hour was spent recording events on tape and tracking down interviews.

Don Schollander, Mike Burton, Claudia Kolb, and Debbie Meyer were perhaps our biggest swimming stars, but there was a young teenage swimmer on the team Mutual wanted me to interview as well, a kid named Mark Spitz. I dropped by the swimming team's dormitory where he was staying, and after getting through yet another security checkpoint, I got word up to his room that I was in the lobby. Would he please come down? My crew and I waited for what seemed to be thirty minutes before Spitz emerged from the elevator. He was a very slender young man who looked all of twelve years old. Spitz walked out, and I introduced myself. I remember saying something to the effect of "I appreciate your taking the time to come down, and we'll only take a minute or two of your time." Standing next to me was this teenager in his first Olympics, with considerable promise but little notoriety in America, responding, "Good. A minute is all you're getting, so you had better start talking." This was one of the few times in my broadcasting career I was speechless. (If he had been my kid. . . .) I remember thinking to myself, how can this young man who has yet to make his mark be so arrogant? Of course, four years later at the Munich Olympics, Mark Spitz brought home a record seven gold medals. I can only guess at how he must have acted under *those* circumstances. I wanted to say "I won't even bother you," and walk away. But I was given an assignment, so I did my job. I got an interview. A brief one. Because he hadn't accomplished anything of international significance at that point in his swimming career, there wasn't much to ask him except what the Olympic experience meant to him, what kind of guy was Don Schollander, and what were his impressions of the other members of the U.S. swim team. We finished. We parted. I've never talked to him since. The Mark Spitz interview has always stood out in my mind. In more than fifty years of sports broadcasting I've been turned down by very few famous athletes, but for every one that says "no," hundreds are a pleasure to interview. Not every interview goes the way a sportscaster would like. We have bad days just like everyone else. My interview with this arrogant young man who had yet to prove he was worthy of attention by the sports world is one of the few bad moments I'll always remember.

Happier memories from that late summer (early fall) of 1968:

Excitement, in the string of victories racked up by the U.S. swimming team—dozens of medals, many of them gold. Fate and good fortune brought some of those good memories to life years later when one medal-winning member of the U.S. swimming team, Ken Walsh, would coincidentally become one of my colleagues at KHON-TV in Honolulu. Ken is a cameraman, director, and still one heck of a swimmer! There was excitement over the U.S. basketball win under the leadership of nineteen-year-old Spencer Haywood. Perhaps he never attained the greatness expected in the NBA, but Haywood was a phenomenon for those weeks in 1968. And there was still more excitement with U.S. gold medal victories by Bill Toomey in the grueling decathlon, Jim Hines in the 100-meter run, and Bob Seagren in the pole vault. Al Oerter won the discus throw for the fourth straight Olympics, and Dick Fosbury won the high jump with the "Fosbury Flop." (He was the first to have success leaping over the bar head first, looking towards the sky.) Wyomia Tyus won the women's 100-meter run, and Madeline Manning won the 800-meter run.

Amazement, when Bob Beamon broke the world record in the long jump—an incredible accomplishment. Beamon shattered the previous mark by almost two feet in a sport that is measured in fractions of an inch! He was so psyched, it was like someone had built a fire under his backside. It was unreal. Following the momentous leap, there was silence among the track officials as the tape measure stretched out, and out, and out! Someone muttered "Oh my God!" Jesse Owens (no mean long-jumper himself) was popeyed. He couldn't find adjectives to describe the jump. Twenty-nine feet, 2-1/2 inches! Almost three feet longer than the long jump in the previous Olympics! An unbelievable leap that no one, including Beamon, has even come close to since. It's like Lou Gehrig's 2,130 consecutive games played or DiMaggio's fifty-six-game hitting streak; it's one of the unbreakable records. If Beamon's record is broken at some point in the twenty-first century, Beamon's mark will still remain a fabulous achievement because of when he broke the record and the distance by which he broke it.

Disappointment, when American Jim Ryun, 1500-meter world-record holder, fell victim to the high altitude and the race strategy of two Kenyans. Ryun was the overwhelming favorite in spite of being ill during the spring. At the start of the race it was clear Ryun was in trouble. Ben Jipcho sprinted off the starting line, setting a blistering pace for countryman, Kip Keino. Keino opened up such a huge lead that Ryun's famous finishing kick didn't materialize. He finished more than twenty meters behind Keino, settling for a silver medal. The disappointment on

Ryun's face as he crossed the finish line was felt by all Americans in attendance.

Enjoyment, while watching the trials and tribulations of a young George Foreman, already a huge mountain of a man. We didn't cover as many of the boxing events as I would have wished, but one match we did cover was Foreman's bout for the heavyweight gold medal. The bout was important because it was Us against Them: United States vs. Russia. Anytime the two countries met, emotions ran high. But when it happens in a one-on-one event like boxing, and the whole world is watching, fireworks are guaranteed. The fight was short and sweet. Foreman beat Iones Chepulis with a second-round TKO. Pandemonium erupted in the arena when the fans saw the referee stop the fight and raise Foreman's arm to signal the victory. Then someone handed that giant human being a little American flag. A proud George Foreman walked around the ring, waving the little flag, his face bathed in smiles (which you *never* saw; he always scowled). The scene was beautiful to witness. We just knew a picture of the gentle giant carrying the U.S. flag around the ring would be the headline picture the next day. We were right. It was in every newspaper and magazine and on every television newscast across the country. An unforgettable image.

And, *Shock and Dismay,* over the events surrounding the winning of the gold and bronze medals in the men's 200-meter run by Tommie Smith and John Carlos. Their black-fisted salutes on the awards platform would also become a headline image that would never fade, and indeed, become *the* memorable image of the 1968 Olympics. Just being a part of the same Games is a story in itself, but my association with Jesse Owens brought me closer to the sad and angry situation.

We were forewarned the previous day when John Carlos accosted Jesse in the Olympic Village. Jesse and I had spent four or five hours in the village walking through the grounds, discussing the events we were to cover the next day. We stopped to eat, which was always difficult because Jesse was still being greeted at every turn like attending royalty. We were preparing to leave the village when suddenly Jesse was confronted by a black U.S. athlete. It was John Carlos.

Carlos was a tall, slender, angry-looking man. He went straight to Jesse and began telling him that there was going to be a demonstration protesting the treatment of blacks in America. Jesse listened and then tried to calm Carlos down. Our crew was standing near Jesse, listening to the heated discussion, but we backed off when the discussion erupted into an argument. "Whatever you do, don't do anything publicly," we overheard Jesse plead, but the tone of the argument heated up even further. There was anger, and soon more than anger. Carlos looked like Bobby Knight in front of the bench when a technical has just been called, picking up a chair, poised and ready to throw it. Jesse, always a calm man, was becoming visibly angry. We weren't exactly sure what Carlos meant by a protest. We thought it might be some kind of a personal matter between the two or a conflict between the U.S. team and its coaches. Finally Carlos, who was four inches taller than Jesse, stepped back, looked down his nose at Jesse, pointed his finger in Jesse's face and yelled, "You goddamn Uncle Tom!" There was an audible gasp from the gathered crowd. You just didn't hang that kind of label on a man like Jesse Owens *in the middle of the Olympic Village*. So, with that, Jesse turned his back and stormed away. As Jesse rejoined us we could see that he was very hurt. Shaking his head, he started talking to himself, "I don't know what to do. I don't know what's going to happen. I'm afraid it's going to be bad." We headed for the car and returned to Jesse's hotel.

The 200-meter run was one of the highlights of the next day. Jesse and I were positioned in the Mutual booth, high above the track. Because of what had transpired in the village with Carlos, we were anxiously waiting for something to happen. The race was run and Tommie Smith won a gold medal, and John Carlos won a bronze medal. Whatever was on their minds at the time did not impede their performance in any way. They were superb athletes with world-class athletic ability. Jesse and I were surprised that nothing happened after the race. Carlos and Smith retreated to the aisle between the grandstand, waiting for the awards ceremony. "Boy, I hope nothing happens when they play the national anthem," Jesse said. "They might refuse to accept the awards."

Meanwhile, over in one corner of the stadium, the pole vaulting competition was going on. Bob Seagren of the U.S. and opponents from West Germany and East Germany were the only vaulters remaining. The final competitors had eliminated everyone much earlier, and yet another piece of Olympic history was being recorded as these three athletes were vaulting higher and higher. The higher the bar went, the higher they vaulted: seventeen feet . . . seventeen feet, two inches . . . seventeen feet, six

inches. . . . It was a tremendous contest. Dusk was beginning
to set in. Finally an announcement came over the public address
system that the awards ceremony for the 200-meter running event
would be postponed until the pole vaulting competition was
completed. The platform was set up for the awards. Jesse and I
could see Carlos and Smith talking with each other. The competition between three great pole vaulters continued and the minutes turned into an hour. Jesse was nervous, I was nervous, and
of course the Mutual Network people were nervous, because we
were running beyond our scheduled air time. Finally, the people
in charge pulled the plug on the broadcast. I was told to sign
off and record the awards ceremony for airing later. So with a
simple "This is Les Keiter and Jesse Owens from Mexico City
on the Mutual Radio Network," we signed off.

I think at first Jesse was relieved that we wouldn't have to
report the awards ceremony live, but then the producer called and
ordered us back to the hotel for a production meeting. Jesse said,
"We can't leave," but they told us we had to. They said that the
engineers would record the awards ceremony. We were to get into
a cab *immediately*. So we went.

We were looking over our shoulders as we left the stadium,
knowing something had yet to happen. We got into a cab and
found ourselves in rush hour traffic—bumper to bumper, utterly
gridlocked. In the taxi, the radio station was broadcasting the
Olympics in Spanish. The driver was intently listening to the
coverage as he drove. Jesse sat in the front seat while I sat with
two other crew members in the back. All of a sudden we heard
the sound of the trumpets heralding the beginning of the awards
ceremony for the 200-meter run. The medal winners paraded in
and stood in their proper places on the stage. We heard the "Star-
Spangled Banner" being played in honor of the winner, Tommie
Smith. Right in the middle of the song we heard the huge crowd
in the background booing and whistling and jeering. The crowd
noise quickly drowned out the playing of the anthem. Jesse leaned
over, grabbed the driver's arm and asked, "What are they saying?" I'll never forget the poor cabbie. He could barely speak
English. He was trying to translate for us what was happening
while he continued to listen to what the announcer was reporting over the radio. We didn't understand. The driver was using
one hand to drive and the other to explain what was happening
at Olympic Stadium. He made a fist, held the fist over his head,
and tried to explain the color "black." Jesse was saying, "Fin-

gers? Hands? Arm? Fighting?" Finally he said "fists?" and the cabbie nodded. Then he went through all the colors, "Brown? Green? Black? Black. Black!" He said, "Oh, black fists!" The driver then pantomimed, putting a glove on his hand. Jesse said, "Black-gloved fist!" Then through still more elimination, Jesse found out that the athletes' heads were down. Summation: the two Americans had their black-gloved fists raised and their heads bowed.

"Oh my God." Jesse realized what had happened and said it again: "Oh my God." At that moment the band stopped playing and all that was left was booing from the people in the stadium. From the backseat we could see that there were tears in Jesse's eyes. Not a word was said for the remainder of the cab ride.

History had been made. We got back to the hotel and held our production meeting. Jesse, silent the entire time, left. As a member of both the U.S. and International Olympic Committees, Jesse would spend the entire night in emergency meetings being held to discuss the incident. The U.S. Olympic Committee decided Carlos and Smith must be kicked off the U.S. team immediately for what they had done. The International Olympic Committee decided Smith and Carlos were to be banned from the rest of the Olympic Games and kicked out of Mexico. Jesse had the painful assignment of informing the athletes of the two committees' decisions. Jesse was to personally escort Smith and Carlos to the airport and put them on the California-bound plane. Whether Jesse volunteered for the duty I never learned. It wouldn't surprise me if he did.

A further complication developed. Don Schollander, the captain of the U.S. Olympic team, wouldn't accept the decisions of the two committees. He confronted Jesse and said, "If you kick them out, we go too. The whole team is going to leave with John and Tommie."

Jesse called Schollander aside, along with a couple of the others, and said, "What are you attempting to prove? If you carry out your threat it is much more serious than what Carlos and Smith have done. You're threatening an insurrection that will have far-reaching effects on all of you and your families at home. Your actions will have disastrous impact on the entire U.S. Olympic movement for years to come." Imagine Jesse's position of having to deal with all these people, particularly given the emotional state he was in. It's just one more measure of the man that he talked Schollander and the others out of public protests. Jesse said, "Come to the airport with us and wish them well. Issue statements that you agree with them, that you object to their expulsion. Say anything you want but compete for the rest of the Olympics. Then go home and make your protest. Don't compound this already ugly situation."

Several members of the U.S. Olympic team did go to the airport early that morning to watch Carlos and Smith leave. The team wished them well, expressing their support for the two and their actions. The U.S. team was then back at the Games to do what they had come to do.

By the time I walked into the booth the next morning, I had spoken briefly with Jesse about all that had transpired, but we had no opportunity to discuss it in any depth or on any personal level. My attempts to talk about it with others were met with uncomprehending eyes. Amazingly, it seemed there had been no leaks. No pictures had been taken at the airport. It had all been kept quiet. I could not believe that the entire world was not aware of what had happened to Smith and Carlos. When the official announcement was made that Carlos and Smith had been booted off the U.S. team, out of the Games and out of Mexico, I was already on the air, Jesse next to me, with the first broadcast of the day back to the U.S.—first television, radio, anything—trying to summarize the night's events. I was going through what had happened, playing tapes of the race and the awards.

Jesse was very quiet throughout—after all, he'd been through the emotional wringer in the preceding twenty-four hours—when the director handed me a note that said, "Ask Jesse to compare the 'black fist salute' of Carlos and Smith to the snubbing of Jesse Owens in the 1936 Olympics in Berlin by Adolf Hitler." It was a fair question—both had to do with race, both had to do with the politicizing of the Olympic Games. And of course, both involved Owens. I turned to him and asked, "Jesse, how do yesterday's events compare with your own experiences in 1936 when you were snubbed by Adolf Hitler?" He gave me a funny look like, "Why the hell are you asking me this now?" I showed him the note. I didn't want him to think I was intentionally putting him in such an impossible situation. He took the microphone, cleared his throat, and began, "Of course, the two are not similar, but I guess I was the only one involved in both."

Jesse proceeded to describe in some detail what he had gone through overnight: his feelings about the protest, about the actions of the committees, and his feelings about race. I'll never forget him describing it all, in a highly emotional voice with tears running down the cheeks of his proud face. And then he made another revelation. "You know, I was never really snubbed by Adolf Hitler, not in the way the news media depicted it. I was summoned to the Chancellor's booth after I won my fourth gold medal. I was in line with two or three athletes from other countries who had won gold medals. I was indeed the only black, and I was the only American. The Americans were performing better than we were expected to—to the extreme displeasure of the Germans. Hitler congratulated each of the athletes in the line, and then it was my turn. I stepped forward, and he turned to me to congratulate me. At that exact moment, a gun fired behind him starting another race. Attention was suddenly shifted toward that event. Hitler turned to watch the race, and I missed my opportunity for his congratulations. The newsreels ran, the cameras clicked, and the media had picked up that I was snubbed. But it really wasn't that way. It was just unfortunate."

To his dying day he stuck to that story. When he visited our home in Philadelphia, our son Ricky asked him, as only a child can, "Mr. Owens, what really happened with Hitler and you?" And Jesse told him the same story. If it's not true, we'll never know.

And so the protest had come and gone. Though it would overshadow the entire Summer Games, the competitions continued, medals were won, and the losers licked their wounds. I suppose something just *had* to happen. Something was brewing. The very atmosphere suggested it. It was the era we were living through. I guess we were lucky some group didn't burn down the stadium. Certainly the Smith and Carlos incident paled in comparison to the tragedy that would unfold four years later in Munich. Having gone through the Mexico City Olympics with Jesse Owens would make it one of the most poignant experiences of my career. He possessed incredible personal strength, as well as an absolute dedication to the cause of the Olympics. It was mandatory to him that the Games go on, that they continue in the face of all political adversity.

And from a strictly personal standpoint, Jesse Owens had become as fine a friend as I will ever have.

Return to Paradise

I give up sports and move back to Honolulu

I'VE SAID MANY TIMES that Philadelphia is as fine a sports town as you will find anywhere in the country. Philadelphia sports fans love their teams and passionately hate other city's teams, they love their players and hate players from other teams, and they are very kind to their sportscasters. I do remember the Philadelphia fans occasionally booing and jeering a hometown team that didn't perform well—but not often! During my nine-year stay in Philadelphia, I had the chance to broadcast just about every kind of sporting event imaginable. And of course my family and I had made a considerable number of friends. Philadelphia was our home.

By the late 1960s we had a house full of teenagers: Ricky was starting college, twins Marty and Barbara were in high school, and twins Cindy and Jodi were in junior high. Lila somehow found the time to start her own business, "DeLila's." She baked and delivered birthday cakes to college students.

137

Parents would order their child's favorite cake and write a special message to be delivered with the cake. Lila and I would load the station wagon with the freshly baked cakes and deliver them to the recipient's dorm or apartment, leaving a tasty surprise from their parents. Of course I couldn't drive Lila on her appointed rounds every night. I was on the air every evening and on the road for at least a few days every month. With both parents working and the five children in school, the Keiter household was a study in controlled mayhem—a busy, happy family.

The workload at WFIL continued to grow. The station management decided to hire an assistant sports director to cover for me at the station when I was on assignment. The new person would also serve as my color commentator during our Ivy League football telecasts, replacing football legend Chuck Bednarik. My new assistant was recently retired baseball great Bill White. Bill had achieved stardom as the St. Louis Cardinals' first baseman. He ended his illustrious playing career with the Philadelphia Phillies and was seeking a career as a sports broadcaster. I was pleased the station selected Bill. He was knowledgeable, articulate and intelligent. Once he learned the technical aspects of the business, I knew he would be an outstanding broadcaster. Of course, Bill would later go on to work the New York Yankees broadcasts with Phil Rizzuto, and is now the president of the National League. But in 1970, he was breaking into broadcasting and learning the ropes.

Shortly after his arrival at WFIL, Bill and I attended a baseball luncheon at the Warwick Hotel in Philadelphia. For Bill, it was an introduction to his broadcasting colleagues and the baseball world in his new role as a sports broadcaster. Bill was quite confident because he knew and liked the people who were expected to attend. But I explained to him that he was now Bill White the broadcaster, not Bill White the baseball player. His relationship with the media and sports teams would be different from his playing days. Bill learned very quickly that he was now viewed differently, thanks to the attendance at the luncheon of my old ringside partner, Howard Cosell.

When I learned Howard would be at the luncheon, I warned Bill to expect some sort of challenging remark from Cosell. It was Howard's style to pull people's strings and keep them off-guard. Howard's comments weren't intentionally malicious, but I have yet to meet anyone in the sports world who enjoyed being on the receiving end of his verbal barbs. Bill told me not to worry, he could handle whatever Cosell dished out. I wasn't so confident.

Bill and I arrived a little late at the luncheon. We entered the Warwick Hotel's banquet room, and sure enough, Howard was standing in the center of the room, holding court. Howard spotted Bill and me, and boomed a greeting loud enough for the entire room to hear. He then made a feeble joke about Bill's baseball career (fair game, I suppose) and uttered an ugly racial slur I don't care to repeat.

An embarrassed silence fell over the room. After a short pause, Howard smiled his trademark grin, put an arm around Bill and added, "Just kidding, Bill, glad to see you," and returned to his circle of admirers.

Standing next to Bill, I could feel the tension coiled up inside him. "Welcome to the club, pal," I said, "He gets us all at least once." Bill quickly relaxed by letting out a long breath. He was too much a professional—and a gentleman—to stay rattled. But once again, I had witnessed Howard at his best, or his worst, depending on your point of view. The man will never cease to amaze me. As for Bill White, he eventually succeeded me as sports director at WFIL, and now as president of the National League, he is one of the most articulate spokesmen for major league baseball.

A few months later, word came down that WFIL Radio and TV were on the block—Walter Annenberg was divesting himself of all his Philadelphia broadcast interests. I was uneasy. When the stations were actually sold, the sports department was informed that the new owners were going to de-emphasize sports. It didn't take a genius to figure out that a sports director of a station with no sports has no job. Lila and I began to discuss the alternatives. It was a critical decision for us. I wasn't a kid anymore: at fifty, the world doesn't seem nearly the oyster it did at thirty. There was a new generation of announcers coming up the ranks. Did I really want to get into the rat race again? This was a time in many announcers' careers when they begin to simply look for a place to "hang on" until their retirement, and I sure didn't want any of that. Lila and I discussed the various options open to us. Lila mentioned that we had always talked about returning to Hawaii one day. Perhaps Hawaii should be a serious option.

Then, right on cue, our old Hawaii friend Jock Fearnhead

called with an opportunity. There was an advertising agency for sale in Honolulu. "What do I know about advertising?" was my first reaction, but on consideration it did make some sense. A lot of journalists wind up in the advertising field. The disciplines are very similar: the ability to communicate quickly and clearly, good writing skills, a sense for the dramatic. In fact, my close friend Frank Valenti was on his way to running the biggest ad agency in Hawaii, and he was no stranger to the sports broadcast booth. Maybe it made sense. Besides, if I owned it, the agency couldn't get sold out from under me, at least not without my approval.

I was unsure of what to do, but Lila said, "I know it may not seem logical, but something in my gut tells me this is what we want." After twenty-five years, I knew to trust her intuition. On what started as an "explore the opportunity" trip, we decided to purchase the advertising agency. We also leased a house on the beach and flew back to Philadelphia without telling anyone what we had done. We wanted to tell the family first.

Lila and I were bursting with excitement as we gathered the kids together and told them we were moving to Hawaii. The

Farewell to Broadcasting

Les Keiter, well-known national sportscaster, has completed the purchase of Len Carey, Inc., Honolulu advertising and marketing agency.

He resigned as sports director of WFIL-TV in Philadelphia to return to Hawaii where he began his career as sportscaster in 1949 at KPOA Radio. The agency will remain in its present location at 1060 Bishop St., and will be known as Les Keiter and Associates.

Keiter announced that his agency has acquired the following accounts: The Colony Surf Hotel, Michel's Restaurant, J.B.'s and White Elephant, Shelly Motors, George Motors, George Sports Cars, and B.A.P. Doc White Imported Auto Parts.

Waikiki Beach Press, May 29, 1970

room was filled with silence as they absorbed the announcement. Then the protests began.

All five children looked at us as if we had both lost our
minds. Moving from New York to Philadelphia was one thing,
but Philadelphia to Honolulu was just out of the question. Lila
and I looked at each other, realizing this was going to be a
much harder move for them than the trek to Philadelphia. They
had been a lot younger then, and Hawaii wasn't a train ride; it
was half a day by jet, some five thousand miles away. I really
hoped this would be the last time we'd have to do this to them.
But we were not changing our minds. The next stop for the
Keiter clan was Honolulu, Hawaii!

I wrapped up my business at WFIL, and in April 1970, I
flew to Hawaii to begin a new career—at age 50. I needed to
get the agency going—or more precisely, get *me* going at the
agency. I lived in the lovely beach house by myself. The family
planned to join me once the school year ended. I had brought
along Shep, the family dog, because of the four-month rabies
quarantine required by Hawaii law. That way, Shep would be
able to join us soon after Lila and the kids arrived. It was the
longest stretch of time I had ever been separated from Lila and
the flock, and I missed them terribly. I threw myself into my
work, visited Shep at the quarantine station, and wondered if I
had made the right decision.

In June, I took ten days off to return to Philadelphia and
move the family. Lila had handled nearly everything up to that
point, including the sale of our home. It was a busy week of
last-minute packing, wrapping up loose ends, shipping furniture,
closing the sale of the house, and doing the things that families
must do when they pull up stakes. Moving week was a blur,
and then we were all at the airport with almost forty pieces of
checked luggage and at least two carry-ons per person. All of
the kids' friends came to the airport to say goodbye. It was as
heartbreaking a scene as I have ever witnessed, but it needn't
have been. Ricky would return in the fall for his second year at
Swarthmore, and Barbara would be back for her first year at
Penn State. Marty, who we had kept back for a year in high
school, was going to be staying with our close friends, the
Buckleys, to finish up his senior year at Radnor High School,
where he would captain the basketball team. So for them, the
airport scene was a temporary goodbye. Cindy and Jodi would
not be back, and since it might be five years or more before

they returned for college in the East, it was a true farewell for them and their friends. They were inconsolable.

We stayed overnight in San Francisco and then made the last leg to Honolulu. The fare from the West Coast was $85. When we arrived in Hawaii—seven Keiters and all of their luggage (on viewing the luggage carousel, Marty said "Good Lord, Dad, everything there is ours!")—we were met by a rented limousine. Piling into the limousine, our first stop, by a unanimous vote, was not one of the landmark sights of the Islands, not our new home or Daddy's new business, but the animal quarantine center to visit the eighth member of the family, Shep. I wonder now who they missed more during our three-month separation: dear old Dad or the family hound?

We settled in. I wasn't the greatest thing that had ever happened to American advertising, but I managed and enjoyed the challenge of learning a new craft. The younger twins were enrolled at Hawaii School For Girls on the slopes of Diamond Head. Barbara decided to forego Penn State and enrolled at the University of Hawaii. She could always go back East later to finish her studies. Ricky and Marty, who were only going to be in Hawaii for two months, never stopped complaining about the place. You'd have thought we had moved to Alcatraz.

In his defense, Ricky had been suffering for several years from a polynidal cyst, an ugly infection that affects the lower spine. He had been through a whole series of operations and complications, and the problem still wasn't solved at the time of our move. (It finally would be six months later at the renowned Cleveland Clinic.) He was hurting, and it was threatening the sports he enjoyed playing, so I guess we can forgive his sour mood. Marty, however, was a seventeen-year-old boy, and I guess that's all the excuse he needed. (Marty would wind up suffering the agonies of a suspected cyst himself the next year while away at school. In the end, though, it turned out to be a less serious infection.)

So, as Lila always says, "Twenty years and five kids later, we made it back to Honolulu!" It was—despite the griping of the boys and the ensuing migraines their behavior gave Lila— wonderful to be back. It felt like home, and it would be just that for the rest of our lives. In the autumn of 1970 we sent Ricky and Marty to Philadelphia and settled into a new chapter in our lives. And though I knew I would miss it at times, I figured that I was retired from sports announcing forever.

My "retirement" lasted for little more than a year.

The Hawaii Islanders were the biggest thing in professional sports in Honolulu, a Triple-A baseball team. The team's owner, Jack Quinn, called me at the agency one day and asked me out to lunch. Over lunch Jack told me that his current announcer, Al Michaels, had just accepted a job announcing the Cincinnati Reds games, and he needed a new announcer fast. "My father has told me all about your reputation in Philadelphia and New York. He says you're as exciting as they get. I need that. I need you." Would I consider taking on the radio broadcasts of the games?

Well, this was as ironic as it comes. All those years I had wanted nothing more than to do live play-by-play baseball, and

Keiter to Call 'em

A very familiar voice to Hawaii's sports fans will broadcast the derring-do of the 1971 baseball Islanders.

Les Keiter, a nationally known radio and television personality with longtime ties in Hawaii, was named the No. 1 "voice" of the Islanders yesterday, replacing Cincinnati-bound Al Michaels.

Keiter will team with young Ken Wilson as the Islanders broadcast team in expanded radio coverage of the team, which includes 30 road games carried live during the coming season, plus all home games at Honolulu Stadium over radio station KGU.

The voice of Keiter first became familiar to Hawaii's sports set more than 20 years ago when he was sports director of KPOA—now KORL.

Keiter now heads his own advertising agency—Les Keiter and Associates.

Wilson, 23, will conduct pre-game and post-game shows in the radio format. He was also named sports director of KHON-TV (Channel 2) yesterday, and will team with Chuck Leahey for University of Hawaii and ILH basketball coverage over KGU radio.

The Honolulu Advertiser, January 15, 1971

all I'd get were re-creations. Now I retire, and it comes to me, even if it was Triple-A baseball. But I was already working overtime with the ad business. It just couldn't be done, and I told him so. "I can lead you to all kinds of advertising contacts, Les," said Quinn. "We'll run all of our stuff through your agency. It's a perfect set-up for your agency!" And so, my sports retirement ended. I broadcast all home games and selected road games for the Islanders. I also re-created some of their away games on KGMB Radio, later known as K59. The announcing job kept me busier than I liked, but it was baseball, and it was a labor of love, so I made it work. But it was only the beginning.

During the off-season I was approached by George Hagar, the general manager of the NBC affiliate in Honolulu, KHON-TV. George had listened to several of my Islanders broadcasts. "I didn't know who you were,"—this was something I'd be hearing for years in Hawaii—"and so I checked into your background back East. What are you doing out here?!" I gave him the short version and told him how happy I was doing what I was doing. "Well, I have a proposition for you," he continued. "I'd like you to do our six o'clock sportscast." I was shaking my head. He continued, "Now, wait. It will be easy. The producer will put your script together for you. All you have to do is drop by the station, read the sports, and be on your way home. For an old pro like you, it will be a breeze. And I will make it well worth your time."

George made it very inviting. In some ways he was right. It would be a lot easier than the three to four hours I had to put in for the baseball games on the radio. And it *was* the off-season. How rough could it be? I knew it wouldn't be as easy as Hagar had promised—it would probably take a couple of hours every day, not the fifteen minutes he was talking about. But I wanted to give it a try. I talked with Lila, and she went along with it. I found myself back in the television business, part-time, five days a week.

I did my first show on a Monday night. It felt just fine. The second we were off the air a KHON staff person appeared. "Mr. Hagar would like to see you in his office immediately, please," I was told. Problems already? Too bad. I kind of liked being in front of a camera again. I needn't have worried.

"Les, I want you as our sports director handling both the early and late newscasts!" Hagar began. "You're the greatest!

I'll give you more money than you ever saw before!" This last statement would, of course, prove to be baloney. The second statement was an opinion clouded by his own needs. The first statement was the significant one, and would spark some intense discussion in the Keiter household.

Did I want to get back into a full-time sports broadcasting career? Lila and I had made a clear and conscious choice for a change in scenery, lifestyle, and vocation. We moved the reluctant children thousands of miles to make it happen. A little radio fun with the Islanders was one thing, but a full-blown sports directorship was another altogether. Where would it all lead to? Another move in a few years? What did I want to do? Did I like being my own boss? (Yes!) Did I want to be an ad man the rest of my life? (Well, maybe.) What about Lila? What about the family? These were just a few of the questions I was asking myself over and over again during the ensuing weeks. As for George Hagar, his questions were always the same.

"So what do you think, Les? Please consider doing both shows. You're going to be the biggest thing that ever hit the air in Hawaii!" Meanwhile, the baseball season was fast approaching, and along with it my commitment to the Islanders broadcasts. My work at the agency wasn't diminishing any, either.

The pressure was building to make a decision about the whole deal. I was actually trying to figure out a way to do it all, when Lila set me straight.

"I thought we left Philadelphia to take it a little easier and back off a bit. You're doing more here than you were doing back East, with the long distances for road trips and all. When are you going to slow down?" She was right, as usual. Life is too short for those kinds of headaches. I couldn't do it all. So what did I want to do?

I wanted to do sports. No surprise there. I took the position at KHON-TV as sports director, and I stuck with the Islanders, including a limited number of road trips to the mainland. It was only nature taking its course when I disposed of the advertising agency a few months later. Even without the agency I was, as Lila said, as busy as I had ever been, but I was back in my element and I was having a ball. Sports was once again my chosen profession, Hawaii was our home, the family was safe and healthy, and that didn't leave too much to worry about.

Hawaii is as isolated as you can get and still be in the United States, and only a handful of the fans in the islands knew me from my brief Hawaii stint in the late 1940s. The only thing most Islanders fans knew was that I was not Al Michaels. There was no reputation to precede me. My laurels with the Yankees, Giants, Knicks, Big Five, 76ers, Olympics, boxing, and rodeo meant nothing. It was like starting over again. The initial response from the viewers and listeners was heartwarming. Apparently there was something in my gruff old voice and visage that forgave my mispronunciations of Hawaiian, Japanese, Chinese, Filipino, and Pacific Islander names. (And I had thought all the Italian and Puerto Rican names back in Brooklyn were tough—Hawaii is like the Olympics when it comes to ethnic variety!) The ratings were just fine, and more personally reassuring, the reaction of the folks on the street was always positive and friendly.

With my return to broadcasting in Hawaii, nothing brought me more professional pleasure than my play-by-play work with the Hawaii Islanders. Honolulu Stadium was the Islanders' home park for most of the 1970s. It was located on King Street, near the University of Hawaii. The stadium was an ancient, wooden, wonderfully worn-out, old salt of a ballpark that was short on comfortable seating and long on personality. It was a typical minor league park that could be found in most small cities and towns throughout the country. It had a short right-field fence with a hole slightly larger than a baseball cut out. If the ball went through the hole the player won a dinner at Columbia Inn. Every time a ball was hit to right field everyone would look to see if it might go through the hole. I never saw it happen in all my years there, but we had fun hoping the next ball would be the one. The seats were so close to the playing field you could hear the managers and the players yelling to one another. The fans could hear what the managers yelled at the umpires and what the umpires yelled back. It wasn't unusual for parents to cover their children's ears or send them out for popcorn if the conversations turned a little blue. Parking was almost nonexistent, so everybody would have to find a place on the street or in a friend's front yard and walk the last three blocks to the game. My broadcasting booth was located in the stands with the fans. I looked right over the entrance to the main bleacher section, and if there were more than a half-dozen fans coming up the ramp, I'd say something about "the fans pouring up the ramp and into their seats." It was like something out of *The Natural*: good old baseball at its good old best. The Islanders packed the stands on many nights. The whole experience was one pleasantly remembered by anyone who ever attended a game at Honolulu Stadium.

The play itself was just as terrific. Triple-A baseball has always been one of the most interesting confluences of coaches, players, talent, and ambition as you can find in all of sports. There are young greats and wanna-be-greats on their way up to the majors. There are seasoned veterans visiting temporarily after a bad season or working off an injury. There are older guys who will never see big league play again but aren't ready to hang up their spikes and gloves. And then there are the even older players who are coming back up the ranks again as coaches

More Keiterisms

He strrrrrruck him ouuuut! In baseball, when a batter strikes out, you stick in six r's and stretch it ouuuut.

He beat the ball. He beat the ball. He beat the ball! That's when a base runner steals a base and is safe in a close play.

Here comes the runner, here comes the ball, here comes the runner, here comes the ball, and he's OUT! That's a play where the baserunner is trying to get to the next base and is called out on a close play.

Back, back, back, BOOM! Off the wall. That's a line drive that bounces off the outfield wall as the runner goes for extra bases.

Back, back, back, and it's OVER THE FENCE for a home run. The action clearly illustrates a ball hit high and long, with the outfielder giving chase, and the ball sailing out of the ballpark.

Wave that shilelagh. That's when the batter is in the batter's box swinging the bat while waiting for the pitcher to deliver the ball.

He rammy-crackled the fastball. That's a pitch that was really hit hard by the batter.

Les Keiter Interview, January 23, 1991

I'm interviewing Frank Robinson at the 1982 baseball winter meetings. He was elected to the Hall of Fame that year.

and managers. The win/loss records and standings don't mean a whole lot, but the games and players do. The play has *heart,* as they say in all the *Rocky* movies. I had grown up, as had all West Coast baseball fans, watching minor league baseball, idolizing players who would never be household names outside of Seattle, guys like Alex Kampouris, "Truck" Hannah, Dick Gyselman, and "Kewpie" Dick Barrett.

The year before our return, the islands had seen the Islanders playing Spokane for the Pacific Coast League championship. Hawaii had a wonderful team led by Rod Gaspar, Jim Hicks, and Bo Belinsky. Spokane was managed by a guy named Tommy Lasorda and had players like Steve Garvey and Ron Cey who would go on with Lasorda to make up the great Dodgers organization a few years later.

The level of play was tremendous. During my years with

the Pacific Coast League, I saw some of the best players I have ever seen: Rick Rueschel, now with the Giants; Julio Cruz, who was a real base-running rocket; Dave Dravecky, who breezed through for little more than a cup of coffee; Tim Flannery, now retired after a fine career; current Mets left fielder Kevin McReynolds, whose greatness was already showing right out of Oklahoma State and into his Pacific Coast League years; former Cardinals, now Red Sox catcher Tony Pena; hurler Dave Freisleben; Andy Hawkins, who later pitched for San Diego and is now with the Yankees; Steve Jeltz, who was traded from the Phillies to Kansas City; Willie Kirkland, who had already enjoyed a wonderful career with the Giants and wound up his years with the Islanders; and the Pittsburgh Pirates' Barry Bonds, who was the 1990 National League MVP.

Rocky Bridges was the manager of the Islanders during my first few seasons as the team's broadcaster. Bridges was a tough, tobacco-chewing, fireplug of a man, who had one of the most distinctive hopping-walks in baseball, owing to an old knee injury. Rocky was succeeded by Tom Treblehorn. Treblehorn did a tremendous job, and is still doing the same managing the Milwaukee Brewers. Angels manager Doug Rader spent several seasons with the Islanders, and following an on-the-air assessment on my part of his choice of a pitcher (I was right, too; the guy he kept bringing out of the bullpen was a sorry performer), he offered me some unsolicited advice on the fine line between coaching and broadcasting:

"*You* take care of things in the booth, Keiter, and *I'll* take care of things on the field. Got it?" (I did.)

The Hawaii Islanders also extended an opportunity to another member of the Keiter clan. During our third summer in Hawaii, we had a party at our home in Niu Valley that included Islanders owner Jack Quinn. I introduced him to son Rick—he no longer would let us call him Ricky—who was home from his junior year at college. "You're a pretty big fella," joked Jack, shaking hands and looking *up* at Rick, who was a head taller than either Jack or me. "Ever play any baseball?"

In fact, Rick had, and he said so. "I'm a pitcher. Left-hander."

This sobered up Jack's joking mood. "I don't have a healthy left-hander in the bullpen right now. How long are you going to be in town with your family?" he asked. "Maybe if you have some time, you could come out to the park and pitch some bat-

ting practice. We need a southpaw to hit against. Interested?"
Rick was, of course. What a great lark it would be, pitching
batting practice for a professional ball club.

Arrangements were made, and Rick and I went down to
the stadium a few days later. We met Quinn in his office and
talked about what Rick was to do that day. Jack then took Rick
to the locker room to find a uniform. I went up to the booth
because Rick had told me he didn't want me hanging around;
that was always his style. Fifteen minutes later, I glanced out
of the booth and saw him walking out to the bullpen in a uniform about three sizes too small. He looked like someone whose
uniform shrunk right after he put it on. I prayed that the players wouldn't get on him. I also hoped the hitters wouldn't be
too tough on him. Of course, Rick had just wrapped up his
college baseball season so he was already in shape and at the
peak of his pitching form. Right out of the chute, he started
throwing his hummers. Fatherly pride aside, he had terrific form,
with a big huge leg kick, a textbook follow-through, and his
fast ball was . . . well, fast. I could hear the loud pop of the
catcher's mitt as Rick continued to loosen up. Pretty soon, a
small group of players had gathered at the batting cage to watch
him warm-up. The players were joined by the watchful—and
measuring—gaze of manager Rocky Bridges. Pitching coach
Larry Haney had Rick changing speeds and tossing some curves.
After the practice, Rick was asked to come back the next day
and throw batting practice. It was an excited young man with a
silly-assed grin who joined me in the booth a half-hour later. "I
was really on, Dad, I was really firing. I looked up a few times
and thought the whole team was watching me! And nobody
knows who I am, Dad, so don't tell anybody, okay?" Typical
Rick.

They had him throw batting practice the entire week, and
about the third night, Quinn came up during the game and asked
if I could come in a little early the next night to talk. When I
showed up he was nothing like the joking guest at my party the
week before.

"Les, Rocky has been talking with me about Rick. I want
to be honest with you. He's good. He's very good. I think he
could make it as a professional player." What could I say? Like
any other American father and sports fan, I beamed. Jack wanted
to sign him to an exclusive management contract for the next
season and wanted my okay. I told him we would all get to-

gether to talk about Rick's professional prospects, and we did. Rick was his level-headed self. He wanted to finish his last year of college and obtain his degree first. Lila was fast to concur. She had seen enough ups and downs in sports over the years. Lila and I were especially pleased for this opportunity as kind of a payoff to Rick, who had lost out on so many sports activities during high school and college because of his recurring polynidal cysts, which had recently been put to rest. We talked with Jack Quinn again and plans were made for Rick Keiter (I think he would have played under an assumed name if he could have) to go to a minor league training camp in Portland, Oregon, the next spring. Spring training would be followed by a stint with the Portland team, and if all was going well, he might have an opportunity to finish the season in Hawaii with the Islanders. Rick was grinning ear-to-ear. Lila, ever the baseball fan, was just as thrilled. And I, the proud father, was feeling particularly good because of my implicit trust in Jack Quinn. All seemed primed for the following spring.

Rick finished his senior year at Swarthmore (he also became engaged to be married), got his degree, and headed off to the training camp, which was owned by Texas businessman Bing Russell, a personal friend of Jack Quinn. On arrival, he found no Bing Russell; he was off on business. What he did find was a hundred other baseball hopefuls like himself. Eventually Rick connected with Bing's son Kurt, explained that he was sent under contract with Jack Quinn, and asked what he should do. "Jack Quinn? The Islanders? Hmm." As bad luck would have it, Kurt had tried out at Yuma with the Islanders and had been released by Quinn. Kurt was in no mood to champion one of Quinn's charges. Rick was sent out with dozens of other pitchers, looked over once, sent off the field, and told he was cut. His professional baseball career had come to an end after fifteen minutes. He called me, I called Quinn. Quinn made a few calls of his own, and eventually Rick wound up in Eugene, Oregon. He played for the Eugene Emeralds, who were managed by the great former second baseman Hugh Luby, leaving the senior and junior Russells gratefully behind. Rick's career was back on track.

A few weeks passed and I got another call. "Dad, I haven't gotten paid yet. All the other players have had two paychecks, but I haven't seen a cent. I'm broke and the team manager says I'm supposed to be getting paid by the owner of my contract.

What should I do?" We wired him some funds to keep him going. Trying to keep calm, I called Jack Quinn. I got some explanations, some excuses, and eventually a trickle of money began to come in for Rick. Rick worked his way into the top left-handed reliever position for the Emeralds and had some very satisfying moments during the summer. Then, on the last day of the season the pitching coach handed him the ball and told him he was starting. Rick Keiter pitched seven terrific innings in what would be his last baseball game with the Eugene Emeralds.

It would also be his last game of professional baseball. The following winter he married Marion Emanuelson, and met his future employer and eventual business partner, David Beloff. When the following spring arrived Jack Quinn had plans for Rick to move up from "C" league to "B" league baseball, but Rick had other plans. He and Marion had decided that they would rather trust the vagaries of the business world to the vagaries of baseball. He was retiring from professional baseball. He informed Jack, he stuck with his new career, and who will ever know what might have been? I'm glad he had the chance to try.

For me, it provided some new insights on all of the youngsters who feed the machine of professional sports. I wonder how many kids' careers get shot down by a single sour opinion. How many have to quit because they can't afford to wait for the first promised paycheck? Sports has always had a lot to do with spirit, determination, and dumb luck, but after Rick's experience I realized how much of those same things count off the field, even before a season—or a career—begins.

So for the time being, I was back to being the only sports personality in the family, until Marty became one of Hawaii's top club golf professionals. It was enough. It was enough to be in a place I loved, doing the things I loved, with the people I loved. *Aloha* is a popular expression in Hawaii that can used for either hello or goodbye. But what *Aloha* really means is "love." And that, quite simply, is the kind of place Hawaii was and always will be. Once we returned, we never planned to leave again.

The Great Tuxedo Caper

Don King, Larry Holmes, and Leonard-Duran #2

A FEW YEARS AFTER moving back to Honolulu, I had a chance
to meet with someone who has become as well-identified with
boxing as any fighter who ever climbed into a ring. I was settling in for dinner when an old boxing acquaintance called.

"Hello Les! Don King is in town, and he wants to meet
with you. Will you come down and meet him for dinner? He's
in town just for tonight. It's a stopover on his way to the Philippines." (The final bout between Ali and Frazier was coming
up shortly—the famous "Thriller in Manila.") "He just found
out you live in Hawaii and he wants to talk to you. Can you
make it?" I told him I'd be down after I finished eating and
meet him after dinner. He gave me the address of the restaurant
on King Street (a coincidence, I'm sure), and we hung up.

I had never met Don King personally, but it was impossible
to not know *of* him. I had absolutely no idea why he would
want to meet with me. I considered myself "retired" from the

national sports scene; it had been several years since I had called a major fight. But he (or one of his people) had gone to the trouble of tracking me down, so I was more than a little curious to find out what he wanted. I doubted it could have anything to do with the Manila bout, which was really a shame, because it was already destined to be one of *the* great fights, and because I knew both fighters. In fact, I had interviewed my old Philadelphia friend Joe Frazier just weeks before on his way down to the Philippines. But it was almost certainly too late for King to invite me along for the Ali-Frazier bout.

When I stepped into the restaurant, I didn't have to ask for the King party—the noise and laughter took me straight to the table. And a party was just what it was. There were between twenty and thirty people from his own entourage and a local contingent of associates, fans, and hangers-on. At the head of the table was the unmistakable Mr. Electric Hair himself, being wined and dined and fawned upon. What a sight!

Even though the light was quite dim, he spotted me immediately, stood up, and announced (it's the only word that applies; Don King doesn't speak, he announces), "LES KEITER! MR. HAWAII! MR. EXCITEMENT! HOW ARE YOU?!" and greeted me with a huge bear hug. And I had never met the man before! I can only imagine how he greets people he knows. "SIT DOWN. I'LL HAVE THE WAITER BRING YOU SOME DINNER! SIT DOWN HERE NEXT TO ME!" I felt like a long-lost brother.

I had already eaten, but I ordered a ginger ale and sat down with him, and the party continued as before my arrival. King was talking a blue streak, women would come up to chat with him, other restaurant guests would send over a sheet of paper for an autograph. I still had no idea why I was there, or what I was supposed to be doing. Suddenly, he turned to me.

"You know it's been a while since I had you on one of my fights," he said.

"Don, you've *never* had me on one of your fights," I told him. This didn't slow him down for a second.

"Everyone remembers you, Les, and all the great fights you've done. And we miss you. We miss the excitement of Les Keiter at ringside on the big fights. Now, I know you're over here in Hawaii now, and you're doing great, but I have to get you back doing fights with me!"

"Wonderful!" I said.

"We need you back," he continued, unabated. "I'm getting tired of Cosell . . . " (which was untrue—Don King used Howard all the time, and would continue to do so for years and years.) ". . . I'm getting tired of Cosell, and we need a change. We need Les Keiter! We need MR. EXCITEMENT!" He said he would call on his way back from Manila, and gave me some more hugs on our goodbye. That was my meeting with Don King. The fight in Manila did indeed prove to be historic— besides Ali's victory, it would also mark the high point of both fighters' careers; though both continued boxing, their periods of decline commenced after the "Thriller." And so I awaited word from Don King.

I didn't hear another syllable from him for half a decade.

Oh well. It goes with the profession. I was disappointed, but more than busy enough not to be concerned about Don King and boxing.

History repeats itself in funny little ways. It was November 1980, and another landmark fight, another rematch, was just weeks away—Sugar Ray Leonard vs. Roberto Duran in New Orleans. Once again I was sitting down to a meal when the phone rang.

"Hello, Les, I'm calling for Don King."

It had been more than five years, and now he was getting back in touch. "I'm calling for Don King. Would you be interested in doing the blow-by-blow for the fight? Mr. King is very interested in having you."

"The fight?" I asked, "*The* fight? In New Orleans? Leonard-Duran? In two weeks?"

"Mr. King said he had talked to you about the possibility," he said.

"That was five years ago!" I told him. "I had forgotten all about it."

"Are you interested in doing the fight?" he repeated.

"You bet I am!" I replied, my voice rising nearly an octave.

"Good. Mr. King will be phoning you later."

This time Don didn't make me wait so long. Twenty minutes later he called from New York.

"LES KEITER! MR. EXCITEMENT! THIS IS DON KING! HOW ARE YOU?!"

"Good to hear from you again, Don."

"Are you going to do the fight for me?"

"Absolutely, Don."

"I've had enough of Cosell!" He started in on the same story from the last conversation we had. Of course, he had been using Howard constantly during the past five years. The real story was, Cosell was calling the fight for a taped-delayed broadcast on ABC, so King had to get someone else for the closed-circuit broadcast. "This is going to be the biggest audience ever! Do you know how many millions will be watching you? Hundreds! Over a hundred million! In Philadelphia, in Paris, in Africa, in Japan, in Addis Ababa! It's the greatest closed-circuit fight of all time!" And it was. This was a few years before pay-per-view cable television broadcasts. Don King drew something like one hundred twenty million fans in to watch the closed-circuit hotel and arena broadcasts of the bout.

"I need YOU for this! I need MR. EXCITEMENT! We haven't had that excitement since you did Ali and all those great fights in London, and New York, and Houston! I have to have that excitement, I NEED that excitement, and LES KEITER IS MR. EXCITEMENT!"

I could barely talk through my grin (brought on by both my desire to do the fight and the infectious enthusiasm of Don King), and I reminded him I had already agreed to do the broadcast, and thanked him for the opportunity.

"I need you in New Orleans in three days," he said, "Can you make it?"

Well, it was impossible. I reminded him that I had a regular job, and the fight was still two weeks away. He wanted me to meet everybody, get reacquainted with all the personalities. "You're my star, Les!" What a talker! He had himself, and Leonard and Duran and heavyweight champ Larry Holmes, who would be doing the commentary with me, and yet he's calling me his star. *Chutzpah* doesn't do the man justice.

"I'll get down there the weekend before the fight, Don. None of the other sportswriters or broadcasters are going to get there before then. It will be more than enough time. Don't worry."

"I'm not worried, I've got MR. EXCITEMENT! I'll have Murray Goodman call you to work out the details!" and we both hung up. An hour later the phone rang again.

"Les, it's Murray Goodman." Murray was an old friend. He had been King's publicist for years and still is today. He's one of the best, a real boxing expert. "Hey, it's going to be great having you back, Les. I can't tell you how thrilled I am.

It will be great to see you at ringside again," and coming from Murray it felt a bit more sincere than King's effusions. He got caught up on my bio, we made travel arrangements, and I started packing.

The week passed quickly between my usual on-air duties at Channel Two and the preparations for the fight. The Friday night newscast ended with a good-luck wish from news anchorman Joe Moore. I met Lila in the station lobby for the ride to the airport. As we climbed into the car we were flagged down by a KHON staffer. There was a long-distance phone call for me from New Orleans. What now? It was one of Don's associates. "Mr. Keiter, Mr. King has asked me if you would bring a tuxedo with you."

"A *what* ?"

"A tuxedo. For the fight. You'll need it for two reasons."

"What two reasons?"

"We'll explain to you when you get here," came the reply.

I had never heard of such a thing. I explained that I was at the moment on the way to the airport. My plane was going to leave in an hour.

"Well, then, we'll make arrangements for you in New Orleans. Thank you, Mr. Keiter." And that was that. We dashed to the car, to the airport, to the gate. Lila kissed me goodbye—boxing was still not high on her list of spectator sports—and she wished me good luck.

On the plane, concerns of tuxedos far from my mind, I thought forward to the bout. It promised to be an exciting confrontation. Sugar Ray Leonard and Roberto Duran had met in June at Olympic Stadium in Montreal. Duran's "Hands of Stone" had handed the young welterweight champion his one and only professional loss, until his final fight in 1991. Duran had looked intimidating throughout the fight, dominating Leonard, winning a unanimous decision. There was animosity between the two men, genuine hatred. For Leonard the personal wounds were still fresh; less than six months had passed since the original fight. The two were a study in opposites: Leonard was young, polished—a superb boxer; Duran was seasoned, tough, ruthless—a street fighter. Predictions for the fight gave the champion, Duran, a slight edge. In the end, it would rival the first Liston-Clay fight as the most bizarre fight I would ever announce.

The King entourage, and most of the press, were staying at the New Orleans Hyatt Hotel, which was connected by a ramp to the neighboring Superdome, the site of the fight. The Hyatt lobby was bedlam. The line for room check-in ran the length of the lobby, clear to the front door. I was told it would be at least an hour's wait to register. People were everywhere, but I didn't recognize a soul from the boxing crowd. Several faces did look very familiar though, and I soon realized why. The day before the fight "Monday Night Football"—New Orleans vs. Los Angeles—would be originating from the Superdome. So all the broadcasters, sportswriters and technicians for the football game were in New Orleans. The NFL brass were staying in the hotel, and of course the players were milling about the lobby. The Rams were also rooming at the Hyatt. Clearly, this was going to be one rowdy weekend in New Orleans.

When at last I made my way to the desk, I was quickly assigned a room and given an envelope. "Here is your invitation to the party," a concierge told me.

"What party?" I asked.

"The press reception. You were supposed to be there fifteen minutes ago!" This was not the sort of news I wanted after standing in line for an hour. "You should go straight there. Mr. King is expecting you. You're being introduced to the world press." This was no doubt a bit exaggerated, but there was a handwritten note in my room—"Les, please join us on your arrival. Regards, Don." Don's note was enough incentive for me to put aside my weariness and head to the reception. At last I began recognizing familiar faces in the boxing world: Dick Young, Red Smith, Murray Goodman, Larry Holmes. It was great to see them all again. It felt like a homecoming.

As soon as Larry spotted me, he lumbered over and gave me a big bear hug. (Believe me, you have not been hugged until you've been hugged by a heavyweight champion of the world.) And the first thing he said was, "Great to see you, Les! Did you bring your tuxedo?" No, I told him. Just what was going on? "Don't worry, we'll get you one here," comforted Larry, and before I could learn more, Don King came up to us.

"MR. EXCITEMENT! LES KEITER! YOU'RE HERE!" Ever the showman. Of course, he then immediately asked the inevitable, "Did you bring your tuxedo?" At least two others asked me the same question that night, and all assured me not to worry about my "failure" to bring one—they would arrange it for me. Before I left the party (with no introduction to world press, by the way), Don rushed over to tell me to meet Larry in the lobby the next morning at eight o'clock to (what else?) go to a tailor for my tuxedo. I asked what kind of clothing store was open on Sunday morning? "For us, they open special," said Don, winking. Then he headed back into the throng, like a surfer going back for another wave.

Finally, Murray Goodman explained the tuxedo business. "First of all, Don wants the entire on-air team in tuxes for the fight—you, Larry, and of course, Don."

"Wait a minute," I interrupted. "Don is part of the broadcast team?"

"Don is *always* part of the team on a fight this big," Murray said. "This event is going to be on screens in who-knows-how-many countries. You think Don isn't going to bask in the spotlight a little? And we also need you guys suited up to film an introduction for the pre-fight show. Don has arranged for you all to be pulled up to the Superdome in a horse-drawn carriage, surrounded by southern belles. Then, Don will stand up and do one of his speeches, welcoming the entire *planet* to the Superdome. You know how he is. Then, Larry will do more of the same, and then you'll get up and say something about the fight and bring some sanity to the whole affair!"

Murray had been through dozens of these affairs with Don and was no doubt as amused by my reaction as I was bemused by Don King's panache. "Don't worry, Les, it'll be fun! It's always this way with a Don King fight!" He shook his head, and we both laughed. At least it explained the tuxedo business. But there were more surprises.

"On fight night we'll need you at ringside by eight," he said.

"But why?" I asked, "The fight doesn't start until after ten."

"There are seven preliminary fights leading up to the main event."

This was new. No one had told me I would be calling the preliminary bouts, but I didn't think it would create any problem. In fact, it would help me get over my pre-match nervousness. "Fine, who's going to help me on the preliminaries?"

"No one," said Murray, "Just you. With Larry doing color. About two-and-a-half hours."

Now there was a problem. "Who's fighting? I'll need to study. If I'm doing it on my own, I'm going to have to bone up—"

"Don't worry, Les, we'll give you a list before the fight—"

"Before the fight? Murray, I need to prepare!"

I must have shown my concern, but Murray just laughed and slapped me on the back. "Don't worry, Les. You'll be great! No problem for an old pro like you! Good to have you back!" and he headed off. I wished I had felt deserving of his faith in me.

After the reception, Larry Holmes took me up to the penthouse—literally the entire top floor of the hotel. It was Don's headquarters for the event, and I do mean headquarters. It wasn't just some staff members and a few telephones. It was a mobile financial empire. The room was staffed by dozens of people, mostly women, most of whom were on the phone—or several phones at a time—at any given moment. Many of them were busy, and would remain busy up to minutes before fight time, making deals for the closed-circuit broadcast rights in every city of consequence on the face of the earth. It was a babel of languages, percentages, pleadings, bluffs, jokes, and bottom lines. The staffers would argue into the mouthpieces like lawyers, sometimes with competitive promoters in the same city. Televisions were set up everywhere, people were coming and going like the floor of the Stock Exchange, food trays were passed in and out of the rooms, and the smell of coffee pervaded the air. Leon Spinks dropped by, then Sugar Ray Leonard. Later I saw Duran. More food was delivered. Every day, every hour until the event, the scene got louder and more frenetic. I've never seen anything like it; I've never seen so much money changing hands (figuratively) in such a small space and short period of time. This is how Don King travels and lives. Simply amazing.

The next morning I went to meet Larry Holmes in the lobby, but was greeted instead by an even larger version of the champ. "Mr. Keiter, I'm Larry's brother. Come with me and we'll get your tuxedo." And we were out the door and into a super-stretch limousine with an escort of six motorcycle policemen! With sirens wailing—at eight o'clock on a Sunday morning—we zoomed down Bourbon Street to shop for a monkey suit. Some minutes and dozens of startled passersby later, we pulled up in front of a nondescript tailor shop on a deserted side street, and one of the policemen, who was larger than Larry's brother, leaped off his motorcycle and knocked on the door.

The shopkeeper took one look at the apparition in front of his shop and yelled through the glass, "We're closed! Call tomorrow!"

"You're *not* closed!" he was informed by the police officer. "Don King sent us here to get a tuxedo for Mr. Les Keiter! Now open the door." The astonished tailor, who was obviously not expecting anything like this scene, particularly nothing like Larry Holmes' burly big brother, opened the shop and we went inside. I was measured, given a ruffled white shirt and handed a black bow-tie. The little tailor told us to come back at four for the tux.

"Noon," said Larry's brother.

"Fine. Noon," the tailor agreed quickly, and off we zoomed to the hotel, sirens and all. The same escort was reassembled at twelve for another visit and another ride back to the hotel. It was personalized service at its embarrassing best. It was vintage Don King.

That afternoon we taped the opening. It was as grand and ridiculous as Murray had promised. The next day was the weigh-in, some interviews, and lots of handshakes with old friends. Howard Cosell and his ABC crew made the rounds. Old friend Roger Penske stopped by to say hello. I tried (unsuccessfully) to get some information on the preliminary bouts. I talked with the trainers, and I talked with Leonard and Duran.

Fight day arrived. Still no word on the preliminary fights—I'd have to trust instinct for those, I guess. I doubted if even Don knew who was on the card. The plan was to meet in the penthouse suite and walk over to the Superdome together—Don, Larry, and me. But of course, there was a change in plans. Don announced that we couldn't leave until his partner arrived. He was flying in with his family on a private jet. King's staffers had walkie-talkies keeping track of the overdue businessman all the way to the hotel. Don insisted we wait. So we waited. Since I was supposed to be the first person on-the-air, broadcasting the preliminary fights that I *still* knew nothing about—I began to get a little nervous. We had less than an hour until airtime. We were informed that the plane was touching down.

"Oh, by the way," Don also informed me, "We need to drop by the recording studio on our way to the ring and record a drop-in announcement for use between rounds." This was going to add an extra fifteen minutes to the journey. I began to get *more* than a little nervous. Don was unconcerned—he had an assistant bring a round of drinks. We were a half-hour away from air. The limo was winding its way through city traffic.

Finally, the walkie-talkies crackled and informed us the

long-awaited partner was pulling up in front of the hotel. Don announced our departure. It was twenty minutes from the start of the festivities. It was a terrible walk, almost a run, pushing our way through crowds. The well-meaning fans kept trying to stop Larry for autographs. Don's partner met us at the Superdome ramp, and of course, Don stops for the usual hugs and introductions. We made it to the the the lobby, which was predictably jammed with humanity. And then the topper: Don turned to me and said, "Where do we go?" *I thought he knew!* Fortunately, it wasn't my first time in the Superdome, so I became the leader.

We got to the recording booth. "Read!" commanded the producer, and we read. Twelve minutes to go. We made our way to the elevator. Eight minutes. We pushed across the arena floor to the ring. *Larry stops to sign autographs!* Three minutes to air. We made our way ringside and sat down at the table. I looked for the promised notes on the first preliminary fight and, of course, nothing was there. I asked King for some names, at least. He said he'd get them and leaned over to an assistant. ABC producer Chet Forte came on the headset to welcome me back and wished me good luck. Even Cosell winked a greeting across the ring. Actor Richard Burton sat down a few chairs away. One minute to air. The fighters started climbing into the ring. "I need some names!" I yelled to Don, and three-two-one I'm on the air, greeting the first of the countries to join the closed-circuit broadcast from New Orleans, the Superdome, and the Fight of the Decade! The bell rang just as I was handed a scribbled note of names and statistics—at least it was something. Tuxedo-suited and mildly disorganized, we were on our way to sports arenas, theaters, and stadiums around the world!

The craziness and confusion provided an apt setting for the main event that eventually arrived: Sugar Ray Leonard vs. Roberto Duran in meeting number two. It would prove to be one of the most unusual and controversial fights I ever broadcast. As stated, the rivalry between the two boxers was fierce; the verbal jabs had started months before the bout and kept on coming until the real fight began. There was also a rivalry at work among the promoters. Don King had a three-fight deal with Duran riding on the outcome. If the Panamanian won, King would have an exclusive on Roberto Duran for his upcoming matches, which would be worth millions. But if Leonard regained the title, the once and future champ would be fighting for Bob Arum and his company, Top Rank—Don King's biggest com-

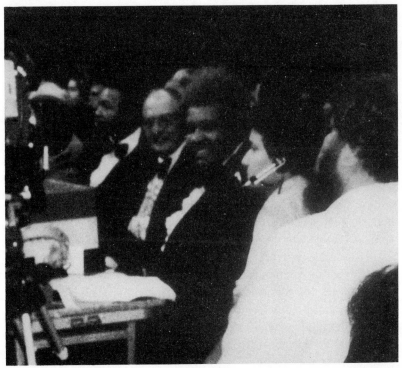

Tuxedoed Don King, me, and Larry Holmes awaiting the start of the Leonard-Duran fight.

petitor. The outcome of the fight would echo financially for years to come. It was a corporate showdown worthy of the one in the ring—winner take all.

Ray Charles sang "America, the Beautiful" before the event, and it was without a doubt the most moving rendition I had ever heard. It was particularly moving for Sugar Ray, who idolized Charles, and it left the contender with tears streaming down his cheeks. On the other hand, Roberto Duran, who doesn't speak English, was completely befuddled by the goings-on. He came to fight, and he looked anxious for the fireworks to commence. But the song was an inspiration for Leonard, and a nearby sportswriter said out loud, "There's no way that Sugar Ray can lose the fight after this!"

The fight started like the previous meeting in Montreal with Duran aggressive and ready to put Leonard on the ropes. But Angelo Dundee had planned a whole new strategy with young Sugar Ray. Every time it looked like the champion had Leonard cornered, the challenger would slip away. There was no way

Leonard was going to let himself take a beating against the ropes again. Leonard weaved, dodged and attempted to stay in the center of the ring. Several times he managed to spin Duran around and put *him* on the ropes. Clearly, it was not going to be another Montreal.

As each round passed, Leonard gained confidence and began to take control of the fight: a little butterfly shuffle, the fake bolo punch, wagging his hands on his ears. He was *taunting* Duran—smiling, laughing, talking all the time. And the tough guy who grew up in the slums of Panama City was not used to being taunted. It made him angry and more aggressive, but he couldn't catch the dancing challenger. Duran forgot about boxing. He just wanted to catch Leonard and beat him into submission. It was psychological warfare, and Sugar Ray was winning.

It went even further. Leonard, who was clearly out-boxing the street-fighter champion, went from taunts to outright mockery, sticking his jaw out, daring Duran to hit it, and then backpedalling away. The crowd was eating it up, and laughing out loud at the hapless champ, who had never before been so jeered. "Go ahead! Hit me! You can't hurt me!" Sugar Ray yelled at him, and he was right.

In the eighth round Roberto Duran had had enough. He threw up his hands and walked away.

"No mas! No mas!" he yelled in disgust. "No more!" He abandoned the fight.

He wasn't hurt. In fact, there wasn't a mark on either fighter. Though Leonard was slightly ahead on points, it was still a close fight. We were only in the eighth round of a fifteen-round match. But Duran had given up. We were stunned by the blunt resignation of it all. I turned to Larry Holmes for analysis (that was why he was there). "Larry, what happened?" I asked. "I don't know," Larry answered. Well, so much for analysis. Don was no more help than Larry. He was ashen, having just seen a fortune in promotion futures go up in flames with the words "No mas! No mas!" King was supposed to head into the ring for an interview with the winner, but he was too stunned to move. I looked up and saw Cosell moving onto the apron, and I couldn't resist one last footrace with my old colleague. I climbed into the ring, tuxedo catching on the ropes, shirttail dangling, and made my way (beating Howard by a length, incidentally) to talk with the new champ.

I asked the same question: "What happened?"

Sugar Ray was no more aware than anyone else why Duran quit, but he was a pragmatist. "Les, I have no idea. But I'll take it."

After the interview, Larry and I went over the fight again for the viewing audience. Don slipped us a note that said Roberto Duran had suffered acute stomach cramps during the fight, which eventually forced him to withdraw. I don't know who the promoters were trying to kid, but I read the statement to the viewers. Duran had looked fine throughout the bout, and looked fine after the bout. Then, a few minutes after the first note, a second note arrived. This one stated that Roberto Duran had just announced his retirement from the ring. He vowed never to fight again. Of course, this would prove to be as false as the first note. But watching the fight world attempt to justify Duran's actions added a unique finishing touch to an already bizarre experience.

There was just one more twist to the night's activities:

Unbelievably, in plain sight of tens of thousands of sports fans, all of us at ringside were the victims of a pickpocket! Someone had taken advantage of our shoulder-to-shoulder, hip-to-hip wedging beneath the apron and the yelling and screaming distraction of the crowd to filch our wallets from our trouser and jacket pockets. As we got up to leave at the end of the evening, Larry Holmes and I noticed our missing wallets.

"Don!" I said, "Don, we've been ripped off!"

And Don King—promoter, hustler, and impresario par excellence—no doubt thinking of the millions his rivals would make off the new champion, smiled and replied, with more than a little irony in his voice:

"You're not the only one, kid. You're not the only one!"

General Opinion

Fifty years behind the microphone

WHEN I RETURNED to Hawaii in 1970, I envisioned that before long, Honolulu would be the home of at least one big league sports team. A new sports stadium was being planned and was soon under construction in Aiea, about twenty minutes from downtown Honolulu. When the stadium opened in 1976, the football/baseball-convertible Aloha Stadium brought Hawaii a major sports facility of 50,000 seats. Could a professional franchise be far behind? With advanced satellite and television technology bringing live events into and out of Hawaii, could Hawaii's potential be overlooked? Businesses of all kinds were eagerly searching out new opportunities throughout the Pacific Rim. The economic success of Japan, Korea, Singapore, and Australia suggested that Hawaii was a natural geographic link between the West and the East. Could a professional sports franchise be the next business to come to Hawaii?

The answer to all of this speculation is "no." The distance, time, and expense of travel to and from the mainland is too great. Even in the era of jumbo jets, it is a ten-hour flight to the East Coast, along with all the jet lag you can carry. A football team would lose an extra day every week. For baseball and basketball teams that are in different cities every few days, the travel problems are insurmountable. On top of the travel difficulties, the added cost of doing business in the Islands is fifteen to twenty percent higher than in any mainland city. Despite the publicity-seeking announcements of promoters every year or so of a new team or a new league, and even a false start or two, I was soon convinced that we would never see a major league franchise in Hawaii, and nothing has changed my mind. It's a shame, but that's the way it is.

On the other hand, Hawaii is the perfect location for national all-star and college post-season play. Promoters have taken advantage of the opportunity. The Hula Bowl, the Eagle Aloha Bowl, and the Pro Bowl are all established parts of the Hawaii sports scene. The prematurely rusting Aloha Stadium hosts the games under perfect Hawaiian blue skies that are the envy of the national television audiences. It's the closest Hawaii has ever gotten to big league sports. I don't consider the ill-fated Honolulu World Football League entry to have been big league.

Aloha Stadium replaced the tradition-steeped old Honolulu Stadium, which was demolished as soon as Aloha Stadium's gates opened. The stadium was the new home of the Hawaii Islanders. Jack Quinn sold the Islanders baseball club and left Hawaii under something of a financial cloud. (Today, he's doing just fine as the general manager of the St. Louis Blues National Hockey League team.) A succession of uncommitted owners followed, and the team's following began to flag. The Islanders' move to the new stadium would lead to their undoing.

When the Islanders played at the old stadium, there was so much togetherness between the fans and the team that it was like a family get together. But after the move to Aloha Stadium, the games became something that had to be planned. Instead of a walk down the street, a trip to the ballpark was a freeway drive to the middle of the island. There was plenty of parking, but it cost almost as much as the tickets to the game. And the fans who had packed the much smaller Honolulu Stadium were swallowed up in the new steel monster. Even at the best-attended games it looked like an off night.

Eventually the club was acquired by Honolulu businessman

Dave Elmore, who went to great lengths—and great expense—to revitalize the franchise. It was a constant uphill battle. Adding to the problem was an uncaring attitude from the Islanders' parent club, the San Diego Padres, and to a lesser degree, their successors, the Pittsburgh Pirates and Chicago White Sox. Anytime an Islanders player showed any promise at all, he was whisked away to the big leagues, even late in the season when it could make no real difference to the last-place Padres. It made it hell for the Islanders fans to get behind the team or to establish fan clubs for individual players. The fans never knew who was going to be playing from one week to the next. Year by year, the crowds got smaller and smaller. Soon, five thousand was a big house. Then three thousand. Some nights the team drew less than one thousand fans.

My own involvement with the team also diminished over the years. At first I broadcast all of the home games and went on some of the road trips to Spokane, Phoenix, Portland and a few other cities in the Pacific Coast League. I was teamed with Don Robbs and Ken Wilson, who were rapidly establishing themselves as outstanding broadcasters. But once I accepted the sports director's position at KHON, my involvement was cut back to broadcasting home games. Later, I got involved again with the Islanders' away games doing—you guessed it—another few years of re-creations. By this time, re-creations had become true fossils in the annals of broadcasting, so much so that many fans never guessed that I was re-creating because they had never even heard of such a thing! As far as I know, I was one of a handful of sportscasters still doing re-created games on a regular basis. I recently heard that veteran broadcaster Bob Robertson was also re-creating the Pacific Coast League Tacoma Tigers baseball games. My re-creations brought me into the national spotlight a few times. I was invited to appear on "The Today Show," "Tomorrow with Tom Snyder," and others. I just shake my head and smile because re-creations were never anything I set out to do, and yet they've become a trademark for me throughout my fifty-year career. As Hawaii radio legend Hal "Aku" Lewis always said: "How you figgah?"

The 1987 season was to be the last for the Islanders, or at least for the Hawaii Islanders. The club was sold and moved to Colorado Springs. The team is now known as the Colorado Springs Sky Sox. The team failed in Hawaii despite committed ownership, creative management, and good baseball. It's failure was unnecessary—a victim of neglect by a host of local political leaders and government agencies who were more interested in grand gestures and gross ticket revenues than in local sports fans and community pride. Triple-A ball should have stayed in the Islands. It was an asset. Fans wanted to support the team, but it didn't fit with the plans for progress, so it was cut loose to make it on its own. Sadly, it couldn't survive.

The demise of the Islanders was mirrored with the emergence of the University of Hawaii sports program. If the Islanders was Hawaii's team of the 1960s and 1970s, then the University of Hawaii Rainbow Warriors and Wahines were the teams of the 1980s and, now the 1990s.

The football program under former coach Dick Tomey and current head coach Bob Wagner blossomed in the last decade. The team ended both the 1988 and 1989 seasons with nine-and-three records. For reasons unknown to local sports fans, the 1988 team was denied the opportunity to participate in a post-season football game even though its record was better than several teams selected for bowls. Not to be denied in 1989, the Rainbows were selected for their first post-season appearance ever. The team played in the Eagle Aloha Bowl against a tough Michigan State team. The 1990 season, after a slow start, was a respectable seven and five. The Rainbows capped their season off with a lopsided victory over Brigham Young University and its Heisman Trophy Winner, quarterback Ty Detmer. For the size of the University, the handicap of geographical isolation, and only average funding for the football program, Dick Tomey and Bob Wagner accomplished a remarkable achievement.

Other stand-out University of Hawaii programs are their volleyball squads. Coach David Shoji's Rainbow Wahines ("women") haven't been out of the national top-ten rankings in a decade. Year after year, with mostly local players, the Wahines play exciting, winning volleyball. The men's team under Allan Rosehill has garnered consistent honors as well. They are always at the top of the league standings come playoff time. It is common for the conferences in which Hawaii's men's and women's teams play to have at least five of the country's top ten volleyball teams. So we are privileged to see volleyball played at the highest possible collegiate level.

Basketball has likewise found success on both sides of the gender ledger. Men's coach Riley Wallace has brought respectability back to the program. His players are talented and a joy to watch. Some of the top collegiate teams come to Hawaii to play in the Rainbow Classic. The Rainbows won the 1990 title with a heart-stopping win over the highly rated Pittsburgh Panthers of the Big East Conference. The basketball Wahines is a team that has improved dramatically under coach Vince Goo. Now if the University of Hawaii would go ahead and build the much-talked-about multipurpose, on-campus arena, the students and fans would flock to watch the high-caliber volleyball and basketball. As for baseball, well, Coach Les Murakami is simply a jewel. Every year, with a tiny budget and an under-rated squad, he finds a way to win. And every year the nation's top collegiate baseball teams fly to Hawaii to work out in Hawaii's warm weather and to take on the Rainbows. Nationally ranked teams from Arizona, Arizona State, USC, UCLA, Georgia Tech, Oklahoma State, Wichita State, Arkansas, and Nebraska are just some of the teams that have played before sellout crowds in Rainbow Stadium, one of the best college baseball stadiums in the country. A lot of the old-time Islanders fans now head to Rainbow Stadium (just blocks from where Honolulu Stadium used to pack 'em in) to get their fill of the national pastime.

I've always enjoyed covering local sports wherever I've worked, but in Hawaii it's always been something particularly special. Some of it is due no doubt to our relative isolation. The entire state is like one big hometown. There also are no big league teams to distract the fans' interest. There are other fine athletic programs at other Island colleges and universities to be enjoyed. Maybe it's the warmth and enthusiasm of the Island residents that make it such a pleasure. But whatever it is, doing local sports—featuring prep coverage, and even down to Little League play—is a pleasure.

People take some of those local competitions *very* seriously in Hawaii. There are private schools with sports programs and facilities that would be the envy of many small colleges throughout the country. There are rivalries that date back decades. It adds to the color of the game, to say the least.

And rounding out the local scene is a collection of water-related sports unlike any other worldwide. Where else do you find a continuing series of competitions for surfing, canoe racing, sailboarding, yacht racing, rough-water swimming, triathlons, and more. We get to see the world's best on a regular basis.

And there's golf. The Hawaiian Open, the Ladies Kemper Open, the Orix Hawaiian Ladies Open, the Kaanapali Seniors

Golf is a passion for Lila and me. Lila and Arnold Palmer just agreed on who is the better putter.

Classic, and the Kapalua Isuzu Open, among others. It's been a joy to report on all of them and be even more involved with several, as golf has become a greater and greater personal pleasure for Lila and me. We moved to Kailua, on the Windward side of Oahu, in 1978 to be close to the Mid-Pacific Country Club, where we can often be found on sunny mornings. As my family kidded me a couple of years ago, I finally hit 70. It wasn't due to a great round, however, but to my birthday.

Along with many of the tournaments held in Hawaii are the associated Pro-Ams and celebrity benefits, which gives me a chance to see a lot of visiting friends from throughout my career. It is almost a never-ending parade. I doubt that I'd ever see so many old acquaintances if I had wrapped up my career in, say, Omaha. Hawaii is like a magnet for friends and colleagues, and Lila and I are glad for it.

Over the years I have proudly volunteered my name and time in support of several worthwhile charities and community activities. The people involved with the organizations, such as the March of Dimes, United Cerebral Palsy Association, the Muscular Dystrophy Association, the Variety Clubs of America, and so many others have been a delight to work with. A particular favorite of mine is the International Service Agency (ISA), which—in association with the Combined Federal Campaign (CFC)—solicits contributions from military personnel and U.S. government civilian employees for use in waging war against Third-World poverty, hunger, disease, and illiteracy. Under the aegis of ISA executive director Richard Leary, funds are collected and disbursed to provide the world's needy with food, health care, medical education, sanitation, shelter, schools, tools, and job training. I am honored to have served as ISA's Hawaii representative for more than twenty years. I hope they want me for another twenty years.

I suppose it's high time to acknowledge someone who has been both a colleague and friend for the last twelve years of my career. In that short time, Joe Moore has become an institution for Hawaii television viewers, and the Moore-Keiter team on TV2 every night at six and ten became Hawaii's most successful television team ever. Over the course of my career, I have worked with and known many wonderful, talented, and memorable people, but I have never shared a news desk or broadcast booth with any one person I can compare to Joe Moore. He has been more than a partner and more than a friend. I respect, trust and love the guy. Sharing an anchor desk with him has been a privilege. Joe hosted a celebrity fund-raising salute to me a few years back, and when it was over, my eight-year-old grandson Chris came up to me and Lila on the dais and said, "Grandpa, tonight Joe Moore became part of our family." That's as good as I could ever say it. Joe is family.

Joe Moore is also responsible for the moniker that most people in Hawaii know me by: The General. It started as a personal joke between Joe and me. Now I could probably sign checks with "The General" and get away with it, at least in Hawaii. Joe and I first met face-to-face on the set of "Hawaii Five-O," the long-running police television series filmed in Honolulu. Star Jack Lord, who still makes the islands his home, was very big on including local actors in each show in order to convey a more local "feel" to the mainland viewers. As a result, I found myself beginning an acting career in my fifties, usually portraying executive and military types. Joe Moore, who at that time was the sports director of a television station in Honolulu, also acted in the series. In one episode I played an army general to his role as a junior officer. From that time, he began calling me General. Joe was the only one to call me General until he joined KHON-TV and moved into the news anchor position. We were on the air twice each night and he began calling me General. It was heard by hundreds of thousands of viewers at a time. Soon everybody was picking it up. I heard it in the ball park, on the golf course, in restaurants, and everywhere else I went. I guess it matched my image, too. I was, after all, darned near twice the age of every other sports guy in town. In time, it became *The* General, and it has stuck like glue. No complaints from me. I'm happy to be called anything that's allowable in print.

What I believe is my greatest accomplishment in my life, far beyond little episodes like my acting stints and the highlights of my broadcasting career, is the joy found in my own family. The greatest share of that joy must be credited to my greatest fan, critic, and partner, my wife Lila Jean. There is an old saying that "behind every successful man there is a woman," and even "behind every successful man there is an *astonished* woman." I'm not sure who has been more astonished by my achievements, but I do know that I wouldn't have gotten anywhere without Lila. She has helped me at every turn of my career. Lila has been a confidant and close friend. She has raised five terrific kids, and found time along the way to be a successful businesswoman in her own right—today she still runs her own company, "Lila's Originals," for which she creates and markets original needlepoint designs. She's the best. And I thank her here, once again, for everything that she is and for what she means to me!

As a parent, I couldn't be prouder. Eldest son Rick is today president of the Spintex Corporation, and lives in Southern California with his wife, Marion. Barbara is a psychologist living on the Big Island of Hawaii with her husband Charles and their two boys, Kimo and Scotty. Marty Keiter, who couldn't wait to leave Hawaii when he was forced to move here, is the head golf pro at Kapalua's Plantation course and resides on Maui with his wife Gail and their two little ones, Chris and Erica. (One of Marty's occasional clients, Bryant Gumbel, now facetiously refers to Lila not as "Les Keiter's wife," but as "Marty Keiter's mom.") Jodi lives in California with her husband, attorney Bill Feinstein and two daughters, Laura and Jamie. Like her mother, she owns her own business, a gift shop called "Burgundy Gray." And Cindy Keiter, after graduating from the drama department at New York University, is doggedly pursuing an acting career in New York City and Los Angeles.

Five kids and six grandchildren . . . who'd have ever thought it?

I wrapped up my many years of sports anchoring recently and now devote myself to nightly commentary pieces under the title of "General Opinion." It's a nice opportunity to share my own views after all these years. And I suppose after more than fifty years behind the microphone, I should have some strong opinions on sports and the sports world. Comments on local sports issues and current events are fairly easy, but the broader statements are harder to formulate than you might imagine. It's tempting to start qualifying an opinion so much that the statement becomes meaningless ("the best defensive player, under 225 pounds, on a winning all-star team during the 1960s"), and it's easy to overuse superlatives. But over a lifetime, there are some players and teams that stand out so vividly, I want to voice my General Opinion:

The best baseball player I ever saw was Willie Mays. Willie could do it all—fielding, hitting, running, throwing runners out, you name it. I don't know if he ever pitched, but it wouldn't surprise me if he did. "Say Hey" Willie Mays was sheer joy to watch, any game, anywhere, anytime. The best long-ball slugger was Mickey Mantle. Forget the numbers, he just hit the ball harder than anyone I've ever seen. Joe DiMaggio was the most graceful player ever. He made it look easy. For clutch hitting it would be a toss-up between Stan Musial and Ted Williams, and for pure excitement, the honors go to Jackie Robinson.

Football honors? Cleveland's Jim Brown takes the medal for running. Jim was simply unstoppable, an awesome athlete. Johnny Unitas showed me the finest quarterbacking I've ever seen, with his pinpoint accuracy and incredible coolness under pressure. The best receiver was Unitas' teammate Raymond Berry. He could catch anything. The New York Giants' Sam Huff has to be the best defensive player I ever saw, and over the years in New York I saw him plenty. Winning, losing, good weather, bad weather, healthy or hurting, #60 was always there for the big play. A special nod goes to Chuck Bednarik, the last of the "sixty minute" players. He played center offensively and linebacker defensively, and he played both as well as the positions could be played. His likes will not be seen again in professional football.

The best all-around basketball player ever was Bob Cousy. Cousy was a superlative ball handler and brilliant tactician. He could beat you more different ways than anyone I've ever seen. The best center was Wilt "The Stilt" Chamberlain, and Jerry West was the finest pure shooter. Bill Russell wrote the book on defense, period.

The last of the "Big Four" of sports (apologies to the hockey fans) is boxing. The best boxer I have ever seen was Muhammad Ali in his prime, and that prime lasted for a long, long time. When I announced Ali's (then Cassius Clay) first championship fight against Sonny Liston, former heavyweight champion Rocky Marciano said of him, "I never thought I would see a heavyweight Sugar Ray Robinson. Tonight I'm watching him." He dominated Liston and totally dominated the sport for an entire decade. I would be hard-pressed to think of another athlete in any sport who could make such a claim. He did the job year after year, first with his speed and punching power, and later, when pitted against the likes of Joe Frazier and Ken Norton, he did it with savvy and staying power. From the early 1960s to the mid-1970s, Muhammad Ali always found a way to overcome the odds and win.

The best all-around team in any sport? First place to the New York Yankees of the late 1940s and 1950s. Talk about your dynasties! Every year they were champions. Second place goes to the 1950s Celtics teams—Cousy, Russell, Sharman, Heinsohn, Sam Jones, K. C. Jones, and Luscotoff. It was only a surprise when they lost.

The greatest sports personalities I ever met were both fighters: Jack Dempsey and Joe Louis. They were legends in their own lifetimes. I would get goosebumps just meeting them. And they were both gentlemen in the finest sense of the word.

The most comical experience? It was a Knicks basketball broadcast from Philadelphia back to New York. In those days the games were sent back to the originating station over telephone lines. The long-distance operator kept interrupting me over the telephone line we were using for the broadcast. (KEITER: "THERE'S A PASS TO KERR." OPERATOR: "WHAT IS THAT NUMBER, SIR?" KEITER: "PLEASE, OPERATOR, I'M DOING A BASKETBALL GAME!" OPERATOR: "SIR, YOU CAN'T PLAY BASKETBALL ON THE TELEPHONE!") The operator and I had a running conversation for at least ten minutes. The New York press had a field day commenting on that particular broadcast.

The most inspiring? Covering the Olympics with Jesse Owens. Hands down.

And what is my proudest achievement in all these years doing sports? Well, I guess it's really just *all these years doing sports.* I'm proud that I've done it so long, that I've done it to the best of my ability, that fans have appreciated my efforts, and that I'm still broadcasting and enjoying it. I've seen bitterness take over some colleagues as the challenges of their careers and lives confront them, and I'm sorry for them. Sports broadcasting, more than anything else, is about the thrill of the game and the joy of the competition. I'm glad covering sports still thrills me. I'm thankful for the joy it still brings me.

A few years ago on ESPN's "Sportslook," Roy Firestone asked me to describe myself in a sentence. I thought for a second and told him I was the happiest sportscaster in the world. I meant it. I started in the 1930s, and here we are in the 1990s. The rules have changed a little in a few of the games and not at all in others. We went from radios to televisions, but either way, we have been guests in people's living rooms. For me, it's always been a privilege and an honor. I've known athletes at the peak of their abilities, and I've known them in retirement. And many, especially the great ones, are as compelling in their elder years as they were in their youth.

I was preceded by the first generation of sports broadcasters, and I thank them for inventing the career that has brought me so much pleasure. I've shared the booth with many colleagues, and I thank them all for their insights and their camaraderie. I've seen and called and commented on more players than I would ever be able to catalogue, and I thank them for it all.

Without the athletes and their talent, their effort, and their heart, life would be a little duller for us all. At their playing best, they remind us of the strength of the human spirit and the depth of the human soul. They show us courage, finesse, and sheer muscle, and we are enthralled by the display. I love sports. I always have, and I always will.

"I promise you—it will never be dull." That's the vow I made Lila on our honeymoon over forty years ago. I wish that every other promise I've ever made had been so easy to keep. It's been a grand parade of people, places, and events, and I'm glad I had a chance to watch it all go by, and even march a few steps of my own along the way. And the parade's not over yet—there are still a few miles left in these shoes. Who knows what lies ahead?

It's been great. It's been a thrill. It's all this kid from Camp Orkila ever wanted to do. And more.

Believe me. I truly *am* the happiest sportscaster in the world.

Index

178